Inspirational Truths

from the Doctrine and Covenants

Inspirational Truths

from the Doctrine and Covenants

Christine Hinckley Robinson

Published by Oliver Publishing Co.　　　　　　　Murray, Utah 1978

Library of Congress Catalog Card No.
SBN No. 87747-389-7

2nd Eddition
3rd Printing

Copyright 1970

by
Deseret Book Company

Foreword

The "Gems of Truth" presented in this book are based on quotations from sacred Latter-day Saint scripture, the Doctrine and Covenants. They were originally prepared by Christine Hinckley Robinson, a member of the general board of Relief Society from 1948 to 1962, as spiritual messages to be discussed by the Relief Society's visiting teachers living in many parts of the world, during their monthly visits to Latter-day Saint homes. These messages appeared in the *Relief Society Magazine* over a period of nine years.

The favorable response to these messages in tens of thousands of Latter-day Saint homes has led to their publication in book form. Typical of the responses are the following statements from correspondence received by the author and by the general board of Relief Society:

"I think the messages are perfectly beautiful and very inspirational. I am thrilled to be able to teach them." "There are times when each of us needs help or encouragement in one way or another. These messages always give me that encouragement and needed lift." "Deep down in our hearts we wish to express our gratitude for these messages. The subject matter is so timely, so beautifully expressed and is within the practical application for all of us."

The order in which the truths are presented in this volume differs from the order in which they were considered by the visiting teachers. In many instances the discussions have been amplified with appropriate materials, including illustrative stories and poems. Each "Gem of Truth" is herein presented distinct and apart from the others and each can be read as a separate and complete message.

These "Inspirational Truths," based on selected quotations from modern-day revelations given by the Lord to the saints of this dispensation through the Prophet Joseph Smith, set forth eternal, unchangeable principles, designed to serve as practical guides to spiritual daily living. They are universal in appeal and adaptability.

Mrs. Robinson is a student of the scriptures. The depth of her understanding of them, her faith and testimony of the truthfulness of our modern-day revelations, her broad life experiences, and her vivid writing style combine in making the messages in this book interesting and profitable. Like her gifted father, Bryant S. Hinckley, she writes with literary beauty, clarity, and conviction. Her illustrations are apt, impressive, and easily remembered.

The scriptural quotations as analyzed and discussed by Mrs. Robinson in this volume are designed to bring faith and courage to readers, and to inspire them to order their lives in conformity with these messages.

It is a pleasure to recommend this volume for quiet, reflective, inspirational reading, and as a valuable guidepost to daily living.

Belle S. Spafford
Former President, Relief Society
Church of Jesus Christ of
Latter-day Saints

Preface

Each generation is faced with its own problems and with the need for making its own special decisions. Our present generation, with the complexities of modern life, must make unusually important decisions. Today's world is filled with uncertainties. Conflicting ideologies and advances in scientific fields have brought new problems, new opportunities and new responsibilities to the individual. In order to solve these modern-day problems effectively and to meet these challenges, each individual needs a better understanding of man's relationship to God. He must have a deep-rooted faith in the divinity of our Lord and Savior, Jesus Christ, and in his plan of salvation. In order to live a happy and useful life each of us must have an appreciation for the spiritual values of life.

Our Father in heaven is ever mindful of us, his children. In order to make sure that we have the opportunity to acquire the necessary knowledge for happiness in this life and eternal joy in the life to come, the Lord has again, in these latter days, given us revelations for our direction and guidance. These revelations are compiled in the Doctrine and Covenants and they apply to our particular times and conditions and have special value for us today.

The Doctrine and Covenants, which, along with the Bible, the Book of Mormon, and the Pearl of Great Price comprise the standard works, or scriptures, of The Church of Jesus Christ of Latter-day Saints, is truly a modern scripture. It is the only book of revelations given specifically during modern times for our guidance in meeting modern situations and problems. The book contains 136 sections (or chapters) and is a sacred compilation of "covenants and commandments."

The Doctrine and Covenants, similar to other scriptures, is diversified in content. It contains many instructions and truths of significant value to all who seek guidance and understanding. Moreover, this wonderful book helps in an amazing way to clarify and to show the practical application of the truths of the Bible. In fact, without these modern revelations, much of the light of the Bible's teachings would still be obscure.

The Inspirational Truths from the Doctrine and Covenants, as presented in this book, in no way constitute a study of the Doctrine and Covenants. Rather, the truths are lifted from their context and applied to our modern-day living. Furthermore, they constitute only a small fraction—in fact, merely a sampling—of the fountainhead of truths that exist in this wonderful scripture.

These Inspirational Truths apply with equal impact to all of us. They furnish us the key to right-conduct patterns, which, if followed, will assure us happiness in this life and eternal joy in the presence of our Heavenly Father. They point the way to rewarding and abundant living, if we will obey their instructions and heed their counsel.

President Heber J. Grant expressed this thought beautifully when he said, "We are the architects and builders of our lives and if we fail to put our knowledge into actual practice . . . we are making a failure of life."[1] He further pointed out that, "The Doctrine and Covenants is full of splendid things with which we ought to be familiar." Then he emphasized an important fact—that we can read the Doctrine and Covenants through and through and learn it by heart and yet it won't benefit us unless we put into practice its teachings.[2]

The messages taken from the Doctrine and Covenants are directly from our Savior, Jesus Christ. If we study them and put their truths into practice in our lives, we will enlarge our understanding of God's teachings, we will improve the spirituality in our homes, increase our faith in the Lord and lay the foundation for happier, more useful lives.

These Inspirational Truths were originally prepared as Relief Society visiting teacher messages, under the title, "Truths to Live By From the Doctrine and Covenants." Due to many requests and because of their broad application to modern-day challenges, they are presented here for general use. It is hoped these short essays will be a source of personal motivation and will stimulate a greater appreciation for the rich value of the Doctrine and Covenants.

The author expresses her thanks to the *Relief Society Magazine* for permission to reprint these messages. She also is deeply grateful to the General Relief Society Presidency for the challenging assignment to write these messages and for the faith, confidence, and encouragement shown the author in their preparation.

For their many friendly expressions of commendation, the author expresses warm appreciation to the faithful visiting teachers throughout the Church who so kindly accepted and so ably presented in their home visits, "Truths to Live by From the Doctrine and Covenants."

To my wonderful husband, O. Preston Robinson, without whose sustaining help this book would not be possible, for his encouragement and able assistance in the preparation of these Inspirational Truths, I express my sincere love and heartfelt gratitude.

Christine Hinckley Robinson

---

[1]Conference Report, April, 1939.
[2]Improvement Era, Vol. 48, p. 585.

CONTENTS

Affliction
Patience in Affliction 1

Character
Character Building—a
Personal Challenge 5

Charity
Charity Never Faileth 8

Cheerfulness
The Radiance of Cheerfulness 12

Children
Rejoice in Righteous Children 15

Commandments
Agents Unto Ourselves 18
Doers of the Word 21
Guides to Abundant Living 24

Discipleship
Who Are the Lord's Disciples? 27

Evil
Speak No Evil 30

Faith
Faithful to the End 34
The Faithful Preserved 37
The Power of Faith 40
"Therefore, Ask in Faith" 44

Faultfinding
    Cease to Find Fault   47

Forgiveness
    The Nobility of Forgiveness   51

Free Agency
    The Gift of Free Agency   54

Freedom
    Freedom Through Righteous Living   57

Gifts
    Divine Gifts (A Christmas Message)   60
    The Lord's Gifts Accepted   63

Guidance
    Seek Divine Guidance   66

Home
    Spiritual Beauty in the Home   69

Honesty
    The True Meaning of Honesty   74

Humility
    The Strength of Humility   78

Idleness
    The Meaning of Idleness   82

Justice
    Eternal Justice   86

Love
    Love Enduring   90
    The Magic of Love   93

Meekness
    The Virtues of Meekness and
       Steadfastness   97

Mercy
    The Quality of Mercy   100

Obedience
    Obedience, Heaven's First Law   103

Patience
    The Refining Power of Patience   106

Power
    Power Added Upon   109

Prayer
    Ask and Receive   112
    Prayer, an Open Channel to
      Heaven   116
    Seek the Lord Early   119
    Teach Us to Pray   122
    The Comfort of Prayer   125

Pride
    Beware of Pride   128

Repentance
    The Miracle of Repentance   131

Righteousness
    The Rewards of Righteousness   134

Satan
    Satan's Buffetings   138

Scriptures
    Search the Scriptures   142

Service
    By Love Serve One Another   146
    Challenge of a Good Cause   149
    Concern for Our Neighbor   152
    Joy of Service   155
    Heeding the Call to Serve   158
    "Unto the Least of These"   161

Soul
Serenity of the Soul 164
Worth of a Soul 167

Sowing
As Ye Sow 170

Spirituality
Armor of Spirituality 173

Steadfastness
Continue in Steadfastness 175

Talents
Magnifying Our Talents 178

Teaching
"Teach One Another" 181

Temptation
A Shield Against Temptation 184

Testimony
A Testimony of Jesus the Christ 187

Thankfulness
Blessed Is the Thankful Heart 191
The Glory of Gratitude 194

The Savior
"In His Footsteps" 197
The Good Shepherd 200

Time
Time—a Precious Possession 203

Trust
"Doubt Not, Fear Not" 206
Earning the Lord's Trust 209

Truth
    Hunger for Truth   212
    Search for Truth   215

Wisdom
    What Is Wisdom?   218

Work
    By Their Works   221
    Dignity of Work   224
    Labor's Rich Reward   227
    "Look to This Day"   230
    Persistence in Well-doing   233

Patience In Affliction

*Be patient in afflictions, for thou shalt have
many; but endure them, for, lo, I am with
thee, even unto the end of thy days.*
(D&C 24:8.)

Afflictions are a normal part of
life's experiences and can be the basis of great blessings,
if we trust in the Lord.

If we keep his commandments, the Lord has promised that we will find much joy in this life. Yet, he has
never implied that this joy may be earned without troubles and afflictions. In fact, without the bitter we cannot
fully appreciate the sweet. Full enjoyment of our blessings
cannot be realized without the contrast of adversity.

Affliction, if we meet and bear it wisely, can bring
us closer to the Lord. It has been said that "you are never
at any time nearer to God than when under tribulation,
which he permits for the purification and beautifying of
your soul."[1]

Johann Goethe once said:

Who never broke with tears, his bread,
Who ne'er watched through anguished hours
With weeping eyes, upon his bed,
He knows ye not, O heavenly powers.

It is by our Father in heaven's own design that, along with our joys and successes, we must meet failures, disappointments, and afflictions. In bearing these afflictions, it is important for us to remember two basic facts. First, affliction is universal. It is the lot of all mankind. Although some undoubtedly carry heavier burdens than others, none who trusts in the Lord is called upon to bear his burdens alone.

Thomas Moore expressed this thought as follows:

Come ye disconsolate, wher-e'er ye languish,
Come to the mercy seat, fervently kneel;
Here bring your wounded hearts; here tell your anguish.
Earth has no sorrow that heaven cannot heal.

Joy of the desolate, light of the straying,
Hope of the penitent, fadeless and pure!
Here speaks the Comforter, tenderly saying,
Earth has no sorrow that heaven cannot cure.[2]

There is a well-known legend about a traveler whose load of troubles and sorrows was so heavy that he complained he no longer could carry it. A certain wise man invited him to rest awhile and deposit his burden in a place where others had temporarily laid theirs aside. After his rest, the traveler was invited to take his choice of the burdens and to carry it away as his own. After lifting several of his neighbors' loads of cares and sorrows, he decided that, by comparison, his own burden was not so heavy after all.

The second fact we must remember about our afflictions is that, actually, they can be the source of great blessings to us. Out of the crucible of adversity we can mold the great character qualities of courage, fortitude, understanding, and obedience. In Hebrews 5:8-9, we read that even the Savior,

*Though he were a Son, yet learned he obedience by the
things which he suffered;*
    *And being made perfect, he became the author of eternal
salvation unto all them that obey him.*

Many of the great accomplishments in the world have
been made by people who have suffered heavy burdens and
whose rising above their afflictions has been responsible, to
a large extent, for their outstanding accomplishments. To
name a few, Helen Keller was both deaf and blind. Beetho-
ven was deaf much of his life, and Milton was blind. Lord
Byron and Sir Walter Scott were lame.

Someone has wisely said that afflictions are God's
educators. It is not the afflictions themselves that count,
but rather, it is what they do to us. Our difficult experiences
are often most profitable if

*. . . we regard every hardship, no matter how severe, as a stepping-
stone to something higher; every disappointment, no matter how
keen, as a means of molding courage; every adversity, no matter
how bitter, as something to make us valiant; every sorrow,
no matter how penetrating, every affliction, no matter how poign-
ant, as something to sanctify and exalt the soul.*[3]

In this message from the Doctrine and Covenants, we
are exhorted to be patient in afflictions and endure them,
for the Lord has promised that he will be with us unto the
end of our days. What a marvelous promise!

One of the greatest blessings we can enjoy in this life
is to have the comforting assurance of the presence of the
Lord's Spirit. How wonderful it is to know that if we put
our complete trust in the Lord, he will not forsake us, but
will be ever near to uphold and sustain us. Surely this great
promise will support us in our afflictions and give us courage
and patience to endure them. Alma, in the Book of Mormon,
expressed this thought beautifully when he said:

> . . . *remember, that as much as ye shall put your trust in God even so much ye shall be delivered out of your trials, and your troubles, and your afflictions, and ye shall be lifted up at the last day.* (Alma 38:5.)

---

[1]Molinos, *Golden Nuggets of Thought*, p. 8.

[2]Thomas Moore, "Come Ye Disconsolate," *Hymns*, Church of Jesus Christ of Latter-day Saints. No. 18.

[3]Bryant S. Hinckley, *Jesus of Nazareth*, p. 75.

Character Building—
A Personal Challenge

. . . one man shall not build upon another's
foundation. (D&C 52:33.)

THIS statement from the Doctrine
and Covenants emphasizes the basic truth that the important things in life, such as character, faith, and testimony
of the gospel, are not inherited from others, nor can they be
bought. They come to us only through our own efforts.

It is true that wealth and material possessions and certain personality and character traits may be transferred
from one generation to another, but the wisdom with which
these possessions are utilized and developed must be self-
learned.

Some of the most pathetic failures in history have come
because individuals, with rich backgrounds and great potentialities, have mistakenly believed they could build on
another's foundation and have neglected to build into their
lives those character qualities upon which success and
achievement can come.

Elbert Hubbard expressed this thought in a different
way when he said, "We are individuals. We come into the

world alone, we live alone, and we die alone, and we must be so girded round by right that no fault of another can touch us."[1] Although we may not fully agree with Mr. Hubbard that we live alone—certainly we are touched and influenced by the lives of others—yet he states a fundamental truth in his profound observation that we must be so girded round by right that no fault of another, whether relative, friend, or associate, can influence us.

This is particularly true in the way we build our testimonies of the divinity of the gospel. Regardless of the faith of our fathers or of the strength and sturdiness of our families and associates, we cannot absorb their testimonies. We must build, nourish, and sustain our own.

All too often we may be misled into thinking our testimony is strong when in fact we are leaning too heavily on the knowledge and testimony of someone else. This may be one of the basic causes of inactivity of certain individuals who depend too much on the support and strength of others. If, for any reason, this support is withdrawn, they find they are unable to stand on their own feet.

This emphasizes the importance of building testimonies on our own knowledge and personal convictions of the gospel, rather than on the lives and accomplishments of others. This is basically what Paul had in mind when he said, ". . . every man shall receive his own reward according to his own labour." (1 Cor. 3:8.) And ". . . let every man prove his own work, and then shall he have rejoicing in himself alone, and not in another." (Gal. 6:4.)

Character is another aspect of our individuality that must be built on our own personal foundation. Although good ancestry is a wonderful heritage and one we should prize and cherish, the only way we can fully take advantage of this inheritance is to take the good qualities passed on to us by our ancestors and make them function and expand in our own lives. Regardless of how fine our inheritance might be, if these qualities are allowed to lie dormant they will wither and die.

We must build with the tools and materials that are given us. As R. L. Sharpe has written:

Each is given a bag of tools,
A shapeless mass,
A book of rules;
And each must make,
Ere life is flown,
A stumbling block or a steppingstone.

Most of us remember the story about the wise master who, before he departed on an extended journey, called one of his servants to him to give him instructions regarding the construction of an important building. This building, he told the servant, was to be the home of a special friend and so he wanted it built to exact specifications with the very best materials.

After the master had departed, the servant rationalized with himself that he could save money and effort here and there by violating the specifications and by using shoddy materials in places where he thought the shortcomings could not be detected.

When the house was finished, the master returned and he gave it to his servant who had built it, explaining that he was the special friend for whom this "special house was built."

Like the wise master, the Lord knows that each of us must build upon our own foundations. Our characters and our lives will reflect the type of materials with which we build.

Let us make sure that the materials we use are only of the best, so that we can build strong, sturdy foundations to support good, righteous lives.

---

[1]Elbert Hubbard, *The Notebook of Elbert Hubbard*, p. 139.

Charity
Never Faileth

*And remember in all things the poor and the
needy, the sick and the afflicted.* (D&C 52:40.)

THE great Relief Society organiza-
tion of The Church of Jesus Christ of Latter-day Saints
was founded on the divine concept of charity. At the second
meeting of Relief Society the Prophet Joseph Smith said:

> *The object [of the society] is the relief of the poor, the destitute,
> the widow and the orphan. . . . [the sisters] will pour in oil . . . to
> the wounded heart of the distressed; they will dry up the tears
> of the orphan and make the widow's heart to rejoice.*[1]

It was on the basis of this instruction that the Relief
Society adopted as its slogan "Charity Never Faileth."

This objective is the same today as it was when the
society was first organized well over a century ago. The
organization itself is living up to its instruction and heritage, but are we as individuals known for our "acts of
benevolence and kindness"? Are we looking to the wants of
the poor and the needy, the sick and the afflicted? Does
this message, as contained in Doctrine and Covenants 52:40,
apply to us?

The scriptures, both ancient and modern, emphasize repeatedly the importance of giving to the poor and needy and of visiting the sick and afflicted. The all-wise Solomon said, "He that hath pity upon the poor lendeth unto the Lord." (Prov. 19:17.) And "he that giveth unto the poor shall not lack." (Prov. 28:27.)

The Book of Mormon prophet Amulek tells us, ". . . if ye turn away the needy, . . . and visit not the sick and afflicted, . . . and impart of your substance. . . to those who stand in need . . . your prayer is vain, and availeth you nothing. . . ." (Alma 34:28.) And in Alma 1:27-28, we read: ". . . and they did impart of their substance, every man according to that which he had, to the poor and needy, and the sick, and the afflicted . . . and thus they began to have continual peace again. . . ."

Our modern scriptures tell us that "inasmuch as ye impart of your substance unto the poor, ye will do it unto me." (D&C 42:31.)

These important scriptures describe for us only a few of the wonderful blessings promised by our Father in heaven if we will but obey this commandment. These promises point out that when we are charitable to the sick and needy we are actually "lending to the Lord," we shall not lack, we shall have continual peace, and our righteous prayers will be heard and answered.

Genuine charity of the type the Lord expects of us must be completely unselfish. We must give of ourselves and of our substance in love, with no thought of worldly recompense. The good we do must be done for the love of doing it, with only the welfare of others in mind.

We lose our reward in heaven if our charity is given ostentatiously with boasting or in a prideful way. Jesus gave us the pattern for true charity when he said: ". . . when thou doest thine alms, do not sound a trumpet before thee, as the hypocrites do in the synagogues and in the streets, that they may have glory of men. Verily I say unto you,

They have their reward. But when thou doest alms, let not thy left hand know what thy right hand doeth." (Matt. 6:2-3.)

One of the beautiful stories in literature that dramatizes the nature of sincere charity is that told by Henry van Dyke in "The Mansion." This is the story of John Weightman, who, according to his own definition, was a "self-made" man of high principles who patterned his life according to approved rules. He was solid, correct and justly successful. He gave generously of his wealth to those in need, still always making sure that his gifts were easily identified and would bring him the best in return.

One Christmas eve, as John read the scripture, "Lay not up for yourself treasures upon earth," he drifted into sleep. Soon he found himself in a strange land. Here he was with a small group of people seeking their homes in this Celestial City. The material for these mansions consisted of all the good deeds done while the individuals were upon the earth, the comfort they brought, the strength and love they had bestowed upon the suffering. Each mansion differed in size and shape according to the amount of material sent, but all were beautiful.

Finally they came to a tiny hut, built of scraps and discarded fragments of other buildings. John Weightman was told this was his mansion. "How could such a pitifully small house be built for me?" John gasped. "All my life I have done good." To this the wise gatekeeper replied, "True, but were not all of these good deeds carefully recorded on earth where they would add to your credit? Verily, you have had your reward on earth. Would you be paid twice?"

Certainly, to perform our charity with no thought of reward or approbation here is the key to genuine and effective giving. None of us should expect to be rewarded twice. Kahlil Gibran observed:

You give but little when you give of your possessions.
It is when you give of yourself that you truly give. . . .
There are those who give little of the much which they
  have—and they give it for recognition and their hidden
  desire makes their gifts unwholesome.
And there are those who have little and give it all.
These are the believers in life and the bounty of life,
  and their coffer is never empty. . . .
It is well to give when asked, but it is better to give
  unasked. . . .
All you have shall someday be given;
Therefore give now, that the season of giving may
  be yours and not your inheritors.[2]

We are mistaken if we assume that only those who have substantial possessions can be charitable. Actually we "lend to the Lord" in remembering the poor, the sick, and the needy when we give genuinely of ourselves regardless of the size or nature of our gifts. The important thing is our attitude. We can supply much with our hearts that we lack in our hands. Someone has appropriately said, "He gives not best who gives most but he gives most who gives best."

Throughout our lives let us practice genuine charity by letting unselfishness, "kindness, charity and love crown our works."

---

[1]Joseph Smith, *Documentary History of the Church*, p. 567.

[2]Kahlil Gibran, *The Prophet* (New York: Alfred A. Knopf, 1968), p. 19.

The Radiance
Of Cheerfulness

. . . be of good cheer. . . . (D&C 61:36.)

An ANCIENT story told in Hebrew households concerns a sage who met the Prophet Elijah in a busy marketplace. The sage asked the prophet the character qualities the Lord looks for when he bestows special blessings. Looking over the square, crowded with barterers and traders, the sage inquired if any of those would earn the Lord's blessings. The prophet replied, "None, save these," pointing to a small group of people obviously lacking in worldly goods but whose faces radiated cheerfulness and kindness.

The sage, seeking to learn the reason why these people had been singled out to receive the Lord's blessing, inquired of them as to their virtues and deeds. Their leader replied, "We are poor people. Our main virtue is that we have merry hearts. We seek to bring comfort and hope to those who are discouraged. When we meet one who is sad, we strive to chase away his sorrow and to bring sunshine and goodwill into his life."

As we think of the essential elements of the gospel, characteristics such as love, faith, hope, charity, and mercy come instantly to mind.

Probably but few of us would immediately associate cheerfulness with the Savior's teachings, yet he frequently emphasized this quality. For example, on the occasion when the Master's disciples were sailing on the sea and the wind and storm seemed about to engulf them, Jesus came toward them walking on the water and called to them, saying, "Be of good cheer; it is I; be not afraid." (Matt. 14:27.)

On several occasions when the Savior healed the sick, he said, "Be of good cheer." (See Matt. 9:2.) After Paul's miraculous conversion, when he was preaching to the people in Jerusalem and they threatened to kill him, "the Lord stood by him, and said, Be of good cheer, Paul." (Acts 23:11.)

Cheerfulness implies having courage, optimism, confidence, and a feeling of comfort and repose. One thoughtful author has said, "Cheerfulness radiates confidence and enthusiasm. It is the antidote to worry, fear, discouragement. . . . Cheerfulness gives mental alertness, serenity of mind, and broadens sympathy. Cheerfulness brings contentment and tranquility."[1]

To be cheerful means to look for the joy and sunshine in life rather than to dwell on the gloom and shadows. To be cheerful means to gladden, comfort, and raise the spirits of those with whom we associate. It means to be kind and courteous, gentle, gracious, sincere.

The teachings of Jesus Christ form the foundation for a cheerful religion. The gospel teaches us to be happy and confident. The prophet Nephi emphasized this when he said that "men are, that they might have joy." (2 Nephi 2:25.) All gospel principles are aimed at bringing peace, confidence, and happiness into men's lives.

To be cheerful is not always easy but it is a truism that as we think cheerful thoughts, we become cheerful.

Someone has aptly said, "Those who bring sunshine into the lives of others cannot keep it from themselves."

Solomon said, "A merry heart maketh a cheerful countenance." (Prov. 15:13.) Cheerfulness, then, is probably nature's most appealing cosmetic. It shines through from the soul like a wondrous light.

Therefore, let us always remember the comforting counsel of the Lord when he advises us to "be of good cheer . . . for I am in your midst, and I have not forsaken you." (D&C 61:36.)

¹Kleiser, *Inspiration and Ideals*, p. 94.

Rejoice In Righteous Children

—And they shall also teach their children to pray, and to walk uprightly before the lord.
(D&C 68:28.)

CORNELIA, daughter of the famous Roman leader Africanus who lived during the second century B.C., was renowned for her beauty, her wealth, and her priceless jewels. On one occasion when distinguished visitors came to her home, a request was made that they might see some of her most valuable jewels. She excused herself for a moment and returned with her two small sons, saying, "These are my most precious jewels."

Cornelia reared these sons so well that they both became revered leaders in their country. When a monument was being erected for Gaius Gracchus, one of her distinguished sons, he was asked what inscription should be engraved on the statue for future generations to remember. He responded, "Simply inscribe 'Gracchus son of Cornelia.'"

Without doubt, the gift of children constitutes the richest blessing, and at the same time the greatest responsibility, that comes into parents' lives. From Adam's time onward our Father in heaven has reminded us of this great blessing and responsibility and has repeatedly admonished us to teach these children "to pray and to walk uprightly before the Lord."

To Adam the Lord said, "Therefore I give unto you a commandment, to teach these things freely unto your children." (Moses 6:58.)

Although teaching our children "to pray and to walk uprightly before the Lord" has always been of great importance, it probably has never been more urgent than it is today. We live in a fast-moving, complicated world full of pressures that tend to pull parents and children apart and to encourage children to depart from righteous principles. Satan has never worked harder to enslave and to ensnare. With perverse advertisements and enticements he is working overtime on our youth.

Solomon said, "Train up a child in the way he should go: and when he is old, he will not depart from it." (Prov. 22:6.) Undoubtedly, as stated in this scripture, if a child is taught righteousness from birth, he will most likely be a follower of righteousness always.

In the teaching of our children we should remember that they learn best from example and experience. The example we set for them is one of their most forceful motivators to action.

This poem, by Dorothy L. Law, highlights the importance of setting the right example in the home:

A Child Learns What He Lives

If a child lives with criticism, he learns to condemn.
If a child lives with fear, he learns to be apprehensive.
If a child lives with jealousy, he learns to be envious.
If a child lives with acceptance, he learns to love.
If a child lives with approval, he learns to like himself.
If a child lives with recognition, he learns that it is good to have a goal.
If a child lives with sharing, he learns about generosity.
If a child lives with honesty and fairness, he learns what truth and justice are.

Agents Unto Ourselves

. . . it is not meet that I should command in all things. (D&C 58:26.)

FREE agency is a fundamental part of the gospel; in fact, a war was fought in heaven over it. Our Father in heaven counsels us to pattern our lives on right principles. He has given us laws and commandments as guides, which, if followed, will assure us happiness in this life and joy in the world to come.

Nevertheless, the Lord allows us to exercise our own judgment and free agency in the application of these principles and in following these commandments. Only in this way can we learn, grow, and progress.

One purpose of free agency is to enable us to develop sufficient initiative that we will not need to be commanded in all things. In fact, when the Prophet Joseph Smith was asked how he governed his people he replied, "I teach them correct principles, and they govern themselves."

This wise principle of living was also emphasized by the Savior in his parable of the unprofitable servants. In this parable Jesus asked, "Doth he thank that servant be-

If a child lives with security, he learns to have faith in himself and in those about him.
If you live with serenity, your child will live with peace of mind.[1]

If we expect our children to live uprightly, we must set the example of upright and righteous lives. "A father and a little son crossed a rough street one stormy day. 'See, Father,' said the little one, 'I stepped in your steps all the way.'"

Experience, too, is a great and effective teacher. If we want prayer to become a fundamental part of our children's lives, we should give them regular opportunities to pray as they grow up. We should kneel with them regularly morning and night, so that prayers will become a part of their very lives.

Let us give our children continuous opportunities to express thanks for and ask blessings upon the food. By all means let us all kneel regularly with our children in family prayer. If we are really wise parents we will, through example and experience, teach our children to have faith in our Father in heaven and to counsel with him constantly in all of their hopes, desires, and problems.

Love is a fundamental part of righteous teaching. The love, consideration, understanding, and interest we consistently show our children will do much to help them set righteous foundations upon which they will build their lives. And as a fundamental part of upright training, we should teach our children to be good citizens and love their fellowmen.

No effort or activity in our entire lives will bring us such rich dividends as the teaching of righteousness to our children. In the words of Solomon, "The father of the righteous shall greatly rejoice: and he that begetteth a wise child shall have joy of him." (Prov. 23:24.)

Surely one of the greatest joys in life is to see our children walk uprightly before the Lord.

---

[1]Paul and Karen Searle, *A Scrapbook of Inspiration* (Salt Lake City: Deseret Book Company), p. 31. Reprinted by permission.

cause he did the things that were commanded him?" The Savior responded in the negative to his own inquiry and then added: "So likewise ye, when ye shall have done all those things which are commanded you, say, We are unprofitable servants: we have done that which was our duty to do." (Luke 17:9-10.)

Not only should we follow the Lord's specific commandments, but to be profitable servants, we should also go the extra mile and use initiative and free agency in doing good and in living true Christian lives.

One reason why our Father in heaven encourages us to exercise our free will and judgment is so we can develop confidence and self-reliance.

An old story states that some of the ancient alchemists believed that if they could find one special element, they could change some of the common baser metals into pure gold; but this rare element always eluded them.

A similar rare element of character, however, need not be so elusive. This important character element is self-reliance in combination with humility. In order to build successful lives, we must have confidence and self-reliance in our own God-given talents and abilities.

Plato said, "Take charge of your lives; you can do with them what you will." In his wisdom he knew that those who were self-reliant sought constantly to discover and overcome their own shortcomings that kept them from accomplishing the things they were capable of doing.

Someone has wisely said, "No man has made a great success of life or a fit preparation for immortality by doing merely his duty," and the Doctrine and Covenants states, ". . . for he that is compelled in all things, the same is a slothful and not a wise servant; wherefore he receiveth no reward." (D&C 58:26).

President Henry D. Moyle expressed this thought beautifully when he said, "We ourselves must act. We must initiate our own search for truth of our own free will. Once we do, the Lord magnifies us, fills our souls with his holy spirit. . . ."[1]

Elder George Q. Cannon expressed the same thought:

> *"The Lord himself will not compel us to serve and obey him. It is pleasing to him to have us do so. But, when we do so it is because it is our choice and in the exercise of our agency. If, then, we should be so blessed as to hereafter reach the heaven where God the Father dwells, it will be because we have obeyed his laws and not because he has forced us to go there."* [2]

Let us follow the admonition of the Lord and do many things of our own free will, "and bring to pass much righteousness," for the Lord has said, "For the power is in them, wherein they are agents unto themselves. And inasmuch as men do good they shall in nowise lose their reward." (D&C 58:27-28.)

---

[1]Henry D. Moyle, in *Conference Report*, October 1959, p. 93.
[2]George Q. Cannon, *Gospel Truths*, p. 138.

Doers Of
The Word

*And the voice of warning shall be unto all
people, by the mouths of my disciples, whom
I have chosen in these last days.* (D&C 1:4.)

Before constructing a building, the
architect works out detailed plans and specifications.
Through his knowledge and experience he knows the
stresses and strains to which the building will be subjected
and that only when the right plans are followed will the
structure stand strong and firm.

Our Father in heaven, the great architect of our souls,
has prepared the necessary plans for us to follow if we
would build strong, useful lives. He knows the pitfalls, the
stresses, and the strains, which are ever present to weaken
and divert us. It is his work and his glory to lead all of his
children to exaltation, and he has appointed his chosen
disciples to guide and direct us in paths of righteousness.

The Bible and the Book of Mormon are both replete
with illustrations of what has happened to God's children
when they have accepted or rejected the warnings of the
Lord's anointed. When they have heeded the counsel of
their prophets, they have had peace, prosperity, and hap-

piness throughout their lives. When they have turned deaf ears to the warnings of their leaders, misery and misfortune have resulted.

The story is told of three fishermen who, unmindful of the rough rapids and falls ahead, were rowing their boat down a river. A young man on the shore, sensing the danger before them, called out, "Ahoy, there! Beware! The rapids are ahead of you!" The men could see no immediate danger and went on fishing and enjoying themselves.

Again and again the young man called, "Beware, beware! The rapids are ahead of you!" The river looked calm and safe to the fishermen, so they failed to heed the warning.

Suddenly they were in the midst of the rapids, and the great falls were immediately ahead. It was too late to make the shore. Row as they might, the stream was too swift and turbulent for their frantic efforts.

Some of us today hear the voices of warning and fail to heed them. We lull ourselves into a sense of false security, thinking all is well. We fail to realize that it is not enough just to listen to the teachings and admonitions of the leaders of our Church. We must heed their warnings and put their teachings into action in our daily lives. We must follow the admonition of James, when he wrote, ". . . be ye doers of the word, and not hearers only. . . ." (James 1:22.)

In these latter days, we have been warned that "wherefore the voice of the Lord is unto the ends of the earth, that all that will hear may hear:

". . . and the day cometh that they who will not hear the voice of the Lord, neither the voice of his servants, neither give heed to the words of the prophets and apostles, shall be cut off from among the people." (D&C 1:11, 14.)

In this day, we are signally blessed to have God's chosen apostles to counsel and advise us in the gospel plan of salvation. These dedicated leaders devote their time and efforts in teaching us the gospel, in warning us of the dan-

gers in our paths, and in helping us build useful and abundant lives.

Let us be wise and heed their warnings.

Guides To Abundant Living

If thou lovest me thou shalt serve me and keep all my commandments. (D&C 42:29.)

ONE of the basic facts of human behavior is that if we truly love someone, we will do everything possible to please him and to conform our lives to his wishes. If this is true in our attitudes toward each other, how much more it should apply in our relationships with our Father in heaven. This fact is emphasized in the Doctrine and Covenants: "If thou lovest me thou shalt serve me and keep all my commandments."

If we truly love the Lord, we will serve him and do all that he requires of us. We will live his commandments and by so doing merit his love and earn for ourselves eternal joy.

In order to do all that God requires of us, we must, of course, know and understand his commandments. Since man was first placed upon the earth the Lord has given him commandments, either directly or through his prophets. These commandments are contained in the scriptures. If we will search the scriptures, as Jesus has instructed us, we will know the Lord's will and also the circumstances and reasons why these commandments have been given.

The Lord's commandments are given to us as guides to abundant and joyful living, not only in this life but in the world to come. Contrary to what some people believe, these commandments are not restraining orders that are laid down to restrict our lives. Rather, they are principles upon which fruitful, happy lives may be built.

In explaining the reasons why he made the motion picture *The Ten Commandments*, Cecil B. DeMille once said, "The Ten Commandments are not rules to obey as a personal favor to God. They are the fundamental principles without which mankind cannot live together."[1]

If we can sincerely believe that the Lord's commandments are given to us for our benefit, then we should be willing and anxious to follow them. Certainly if we are wise we will follow these rules and principles, which, as it has been proven down through the ages, will assure us satisfaction, peace, and joy.

The Doctrine and Covenants quotation emphasizes the fact that to lay the foundation for an effective life we must keep *all* of the Lord's commandments. This means that we do not have the privilege to choose only those that appeal to us.

It also means that we must not concentrate just upon the Lord's major commandments, such as those given and recorded by Moses. We must be conscious of the many little commandments that do so much to make others happy and which reflect strength in our own characters. Furthermore, we must not put greater emphasis on some commandments at the expense of others.

This fact was beautifully dramatized by the Savior when he answered the rich young man who inquired of him what he should do to inherit eternal life. Jesus replied,

"Thou knowest the commandments, Do not commit adultery, Do not kill, Do not steal, Do not bear false witness, Defraud not, Honour thy father and mother.

"And he answered and said unto him, Master, all these have I observed from my youth.

"Then Jesus beholding him loved him, and said unto him, One thing thou lackest: go thy way, sell whatsoever thou hast, and give to the poor, and thou shalt have treasure in heaven: and come, . . . follow me.

"And he was sad at the saying, and went away grieved; for he had great possessions." (Mark 10:19-22.)

The scriptures do not complete the story and tell us what happened to this young man who did not have the courage to live all of God's commandments. We can be sure, however, that had he possessed the strength to follow Jesus, he would have had treasures in heaven and would have been greatly blessed.

Even the strongest of us may at times find ourselves thinking that it is difficult to obey certain of the Lord's commandments. When we encounter these difficulties, we can take comfort in the fact that the Lord does not ask anything of us without preparing the way for us to do that which he requires. This fact was expressed by the Book of Mormon prophet Nephi when he said: ". . . I will go and do the things which the Lord hath commanded, for I know that the Lord giveth no commandments unto the children of men, save he shall prepare a way for them that they may accomplish the thing which he commandeth them." (1 Nephi 3:7.)

If we will hold fast to this conviction, we will always have the courage and the strength to do whatever the Lord asks us to do.

When we keep the Lord's commandments, we truly serve him. Furthermore, as recorded by the beloved apostle John, "He that hath my commandments, and keepeth them, he it is that loveth me: and he that loveth me shall be loved of my Father, and I will love him. . . ." (John 14:21.)

---

[1]*Instructor*, August 1957, p. 231.

Who Are The Lord's Disciples?

He that receiveth my law and doeth it, the same is my disciple. . . . (D&C 41:5.)

A DISCIPLE is a student and follower of his master's teachings. To be Christ's disciples, we must study and understand the Savior's teachings and put them into effect in our lives.

The great blessing that comes to the Savior's disciples is the marvelous opportunity to have the assistance of his Spirit. Those who enjoy the presence of his Spirit have peace of mind. They are given the power to meet and overcome life's problems and, through his help, enjoy the satisfactions of achieving great accomplishments in the service of others.

How can we become Christ's disciples? He has told us, "He that receiveth my law and doeth it, the same is my disciple. . . ."

The first step, then, in becoming his disciple is to know, understand, and receive his law. The Savior's laws are the laws of the gospel. They are the teachings he gave us during his life here upon the earth. They are also the teachings and commandments given by inspiration and revelation to all of his prophets, both ancient and modern, as found in the scriptures and in our leaders' present-day instructions.

Understanding and receiving the Savior's laws constitute a continuous and lifetime challenge and opportunity. We must never cease studying and learning.

Receiving the law, however, is not enough. We must put the law into action in our lives. The Book of Mormon prophet, King Benjamin, clearly expressed this truth when he said, ". . . and now, if you believe all these things see that ye do them." (Mosiah 4:10.) The apostle James expressed this thought when he said, "But be ye doers of the word, and not hearers only, deceiving your own selves." (James 1:22.)

The gospel of Jesus Christ is a gospel of work. We know that through our good works we will be saved, and by our desires and works we will be judged.

An ancient fable tells of a certain farmer who had three friends. Two of these friends he held in high esteem and associated with constantly. The third, although of genuine character, was neglected by the farmer.

Accused wrongfully before the law, the farmer was summoned to court. He needed a character witness and went first to his preferred friends. The first of these gave many reasons why he could not present himself at court. The second friend was willing to accompany him, but could go no further than the door. The third, whom he had least esteemed, not only did accompany the farmer but so ably defended him before the judge that he was acquitted.

According to this fable, each individual during his lifetime makes three friends. These are his worldly possessions, his family and neighbors, and his good works. When he leaves this life and faces the Great Judge, his first friend, worldly possessions, must be left behind. The second friend, his family and neighbors, can accompany him only to death's door. His third friend, however, the one he is inclined to neglect—his good works—is the only one who can go with him and help him to plead his cause.

A true disciple of the Savior is a performer of good works. He knows that by his works he will be judged. He not only receives Christ's words but puts them into action and writes them upon the table of his heart. (See Prov. 3:3.)

Jesus described a true disciple when he said:

Therefore whosoever heareth these sayings of mine, and doeth them, I will liken him unto a wise man, which built his house upon a rock. (Matt. 7:24.)

Let us all earn the rich blessings that come to true disciples of our Lord.

Speak No Evil

Thou shalt not speak evil of thy neighbor, nor do him any harm. (D&C 42:27.)

THIS wise counsel comes from the section of the Doctrine and Covenants that was described by Joseph Smith as embracing the law of the Church. To avoid speaking evil of one's neighbor and to make sure that we do him no harm is also a fundamental law of intelligent human behavior. If, in our personal contacts with others, we want to spread love, friendship, understanding, and good will, we must practice this principle.

The story is told of a man who had circulated slanderous gossip about a neighbor only to find the story was not true. Conscience-stricken, the man sought the advice of a friend to see what could be done to retrieve the evil words he had spoken. His wise friend told him to take a bag filled with goose feathers and to drop a handful of feathers at each door in the village.

The man followed this advice and returned to his friend for further instructions.

"Now take your bag to each house once more," replied the friend, "and gather up each goose feather you have dropped."

The man sadly shook his head and said, "That I cannot do, for the wind has scattered them over the countryside."

Like these scattered feathers, gossip and unkind words are almost impossible to retrieve. Regardless of how we may try to take them back and even if we sincerely repent, it may be impossible to undo the harm that has been inflicted. This is true of any type of slanderous or misrepresented statement.

All of us have two words in our vocabularies that can be easily and lightly spoken to spread rumor or a bit of gossip. These two words are "they say." These are innocent words rarely spoken deliberately to do harm; but when they preface even the most casual remark that might misrepresent or undermine the character of another, they can do damage that may never be fully repaired.

Down through the ages, the Lord has been much concerned about the human tendency "to speak ill of others." Through his prophet Solomon, we are reminded that five of the seven things that "the Lord hates" are actions associated with speaking evil and doing harm to our neighbors. The five are "a lying tongue, . . . An heart that deviseth wicked imaginations, feet that be swift in running to mischief, A false witness that speaketh lies, and he that soweth discord among brethren." (Prov. 6:16-19.)

Jesus added force to this warning when he said, ". . . every idle word that men speak, they shall give account thereof in the day of judgment. For by thy words thou shalt be justified, and by thy words thou shalt be condemned." (Matt. 12:36-37.)

He also gave us the key to our personal responsibility in this respect when he said, ". . . how canst thou say to thy brother, Brother, let me pull out the mote that is in thine eye, when thou thyself beholdest not the beam that is in thine own eye? . . ." (Luke 6:42.)

One of our LDS hymns also advises us,

Should you feel inclined to censure
Faults you may in others view,
Ask your own heart, e're you venture,
If thou hast not failings too.[1]

Someone has wisely said, "No man in the world ever attempted to wrong another without being injured in return. Nature keeps her books well; she puts down every item, she closes all accounts. Not always at the end of each month but sometime, somewhere."

Our best assurance that we can fulfill the commandment given to us in the Doctrine and Covenants quotation will come to us only if we fill our minds and hearts so full with appreciation, love, understanding, and friendliness toward each other that these good thoughts and good works will stifle and crowd out any temptation to speak ill of another.

A much-loved woman was once asked how she was able to attract and hold so many true friends. She replied, "I have made it a practice never to speak ill of another. When I see someone make a mistake, I try always to say to myself, had I faced similar circumstances I might have done worse."

The Prophet Joseph Smith, in talking to the first Relief Society, said: "Don't be limited in your views with regard to your neighbors' virtues. . . . You must enlarge your souls toward each other. . . . You must be long-suffering and bear with the faults and errors of mankind. . . . Be liberal in your feelings. . . . Let kindness, charity and love crown your works."[2]

Let us heed this commandment in the Doctrine and Covenants. Rather than speaking ill, let us oft speak kind words of and to each other, for "kind words are sweet tones of the heart."

---

[1]Phillip Paul Bliss, "Should You Feel Inclined to Censure," *Hymns*, Church of Jesus Christ of Latter-day Saints, No. 159.

[2]*Documentary History of the Church*, Vol. 4, pp. 602-7.

Faithful
Unto The End

Be faithful unto the end, and lo, I am with you. . . . (D&C 31:13.)

I<small>T</small> IS a rule of life that each of us, along with joy, success, and accomplishments, must meet our share of trials, troubles, disappointments, and temptations. One of the reasons we are put on this earth is for us to learn how to stand firm and strong against these buffetings.

At no time should we boast we are saved. As long as we live, we are subject to the possible temptations of Satan. This is a fundamental part of the great plan of salvation. Neither can we at any time hope to sit back and rest upon past successes and achievements. We either progress and grow or we slip backwards.

The Lord hopes we will live joyously, courageously, and enthusiastically all the days of our life. We are promised that if we do this, we shall receive rich, eternal blessings. In the Book of Mormon, King Benjamin says: ". . . if they hold out faithful to the end they are received into heaven, . . . for the Lord God hath spoken it." (Mosiah 2:41.) The Prophet Nephi declared: ". . . if they endure until the end they shall be lifted up at the last day." (1 Nephi 13:37.)

In the New Testament the Lord has promised that "he that endureth to the end shall be saved." (Matt. 10:22.) And again, in the Book of Revalations, the Savior said, ". . . be thou faithful unto death, and I will give thee a crown of life." (Rev. 2:10.)

As we ponder this truth, "Be faithful unto the end, and lo I am with you," let us remember that "these words are not of man . . . but of me, even Jesus Christ, your Redeemer, by the will of the Father." (D&C 31:13.)

It is an encouraging fact that the Lord gives us no commandment nor admonition that is beyond our ability to obey. The commandment, "To be faithful unto the end," may at first glance seem to be an extremely severe one. We know our own weaknesses and the ease with which we can succumb to them. Furthermore, we never know under what circumstances or when our own end will come. How, then, can we be constantly faithful?

President Heber J. Grant gave us an explicit answer. He said, "Let us all do the will of our Father in heaven today, and we will then be prepared for the duty of tomorrow and for the eternities to come."[1]

Being faithful unto the end consists simply in meeting each day's problems and temptations constructively and righteously as they come. One of the beautiful, encouraging aspects of life's experiences is that each problem met and surmounted strengthens us to meet the next. If we approach them intelligently, all of life's experiences, good or bad, can serve as steppingstones to a stronger, more stalwart character.

Many of the influences that divert us from constant faithfulness are not the big problems but life's little temptations. In the western part of the United States stands a forest of trees that for centuries have withstood the rigors of winds and storms. Today, despite their stalwart heights and sturdy roots, they are slowly but surely dying. Minute worms have worked their way under the bark and into the hearts of the trees. These little termites are killing trees that for centuries have withstood mighty storms.

So it is with life. Often it is the little temptations that enter into our souls and weaken our resistance. Some of these destroying influences consist of such things as greed, falsehood, deception, shortness of temper, arrogance, jealousy, faultfinding, slander, intolerance, and false pride.

If we guard against these little weaknesses and meet each problem honestly, courageously, as it comes, recognizing that none of us can see the end from the beginning, then the Savior has assured us that he will be with us and will help us to endure to the end. He has promised: "Be faithful unto the end, and lo, I am with you."

If we continue in faithfulness and endure to the end, then we too can say, as did the apostle Paul of old, "I have fought a good fight, I have finished my course, I have kept the faith:

"Henceforth there is laid up for me a crown of righteousness, which the Lord, the righteous judge, shall give me at that day. . . ." (2 Tim. 4:7-8.)

---

[1]Theme of the Mutual Improvement Associations, 1943-44.

The Faithful
Preserved

And inasmuch as they are faithful they
shall be preserved, and I, the Lord, will
be with them. (D&C 61:10.)

THE SCRIPTURES are filled with promises that those who remain steadfast and faithful to the Lord's commandments shall be protected and preserved. David the Psalmist said, "For the Lord . . . forsaketh not his saints; they are preserved forever. . . ." (Ps. 37:28.) The great general and prophet Moroni in the Book of Mormon declared, ". . . God will support, and keep, and preserve us, so long as we are faithful unto him. . . ." (Alma 44:4.)

There are both physical and spiritual aspects to the Lord's promises and assurances that the faithful will be guarded, saved, and preserved. In some instances, the faithful will be protected and preserved against physical harm. This was the meaning of this promise given by Moroni.

More frequently, however, this promise has had a spiritual rather than a physical meaning. The statement given above by David had this more enduring meaning.

He spoke of the faithful people being preserved not just in this life but "forever."

It is this broader meaning that the Savior emphasized when he said, "Whosoever shall seek to save his life shall lose it; and whosoever shall lose his life shall preserve it." (Luke 17:33.) Obviously, when one loses his life, as indicated in this scripture, he is not preserved and protected physically; yet, as the Savior has promised, if one loses himself, and even his life, in the service of others, and thereby in the Lord's service, he preserves his soul and gains eternal life.

Over and over again the Savior emphasized the divine fact that saving one's soul is infinitely more important than preserving one's life. "For what shall it profit a man, if he shall gain the whole world, and lose his own soul?" (Mark 8:36.)

To be preserved in a spiritual sense means to be delivered from evil; to be shielded by the Lord's spirit; to be secure and firm in our convictions of the truth. It means to be sustained and upheld in reighteousness, and to possess one of the Lord's choice gifts, the blessing of peace of mind.

Temple Bailey, in an impressive story, tells about a young mother who set her foot on the path of life and wondered if the way would be long and hard. Her guide said to her, "Yes, the way is hard and you will be old before you reach the end of it, but the end will be better than the beginning."

In this story the young mother faced her problems with faith and confidence; but as her children grew, illness came into their lives, and there was sorrow, and the way was stormy and dark. The children were filled with fear and uncertainty, but they came to their mother with confidence, and she covered them with her protective mantle of love. Then the mother said to her guide, "These days are even better than the brightness of the sun, for now my children have learned courage."

This story continues with the experiences of trouble and affliction through which the mother and her children learned the true meaning of faith and love and the need for the constant assurance of the Lord's protective spirit. They learned that with faithfulness through life's experiences, both bitter and sweet, the Lord helped them to develop the qualities that preserved their spiritual strength, and thus they came to realize that the end was better than the beginning.

President Hugh B. Brown said:

> *Men sometimes labor under the false impression that reverses, disappointments, tragedies come only as a result of sin and disobedience. . . . The trial perhaps may come . . . to teach some of the great lessons of life. And so we must remember that the winds blow and the rains beat upon the house that is built upon the rock. The promise is not exemption from the storm but that they who shall so build shall have strength to withstand it.*[1]

We will not be spared from the problems of life and we may not be spared from some of its tragedies. But the Lord will give us his protective spirit as a shield. His strength will become our strength.

If we are truly faithful, we have no need to fear, for we can have the Lord's comforting Spirit to be with us and his assurance that our souls will be preserved throughout this life and eternity.

---

[1]Hugh B. Brown, *The Eternal Quest* (Salt Lake City: Bookcraft), pp. 247-48.

The Power
Of Faith

*. . . according to men's faith it shall be
done unto them.* (D&C 52:20.)

THROUGHOUT the scriptures, both
ancient and modern, no truth is emphasized more repeatedly and clearly than the promise that the Lord will
bestow blessings upon us according to our faith. Since the
days of Adam, God's children have been admonished to
"walk by faith," in the solution of all their problems.
They have been urged to take advantage of this limitless
reservoir of power. So great is the power of this principle
that the Lord has said, " . . . If ye have faith as a grain
of mustard seed, ye shall say unto this mountain, remove
hence . . . and it shall remove; and nothing shall be impossible unto you." (Matt. 17:20.)

The scriptures are replete with outstanding examples
of remarkable faith. The stories of Abraham and of Lehi
both echo this absolute conviction. "By faith, Abraham,
when he was called to go out into a place . . . went out,
not knowing whither he went." (Heb. 11:8.) Lehi, in
obedience unto the word of the Lord, took his family and

departed into the wilderness, leaving the land of his inheritance, his home, his gold and silver and precious
things.

In the Old Testament, events are described how,
through the power of faith, Moses led the children of
Israel through the parted waters of the Red Sea; how
David vanquished Goliath and saved his people from
destruction; and how the Lord shut the mouths of the
lions and saved his prophet Daniel.

The New Testament and the Book of Mormon have
many accounts of the great miracles the Savior and his
disciples wrought through their faith and through the faith
of the people who were thus blessed. Through faith the
sick were healed, the blind were given sight, and the
dead were brought back to life.

Among the many examples of the power of faith in
the Book of Mormon, two particularly stand out. One is
the story of Helaman and his two thousand warriors, sons
of Nephite mothers. These young men fought a great and
victorious battle against the Lamanites and not one soul
perished, because of their exceeding great faith in that
which their mothers had taught them. (Alma 57:26.) Another example is the story of the brother of Jared, whose
faith was so exceedingly great that the veil was taken
from his eyes and he saw the finger of the Lord, and the
Lord himself. (Ether 12:4.)

In modern times the wonderful power of this great
principle was magnificently exemplified in the simple
prayer offered with unwavering faith by Joseph Smith,
when he asked the Lord for wisdom and beheld the Father
and the Son in a glorious vision.

This same source of power that brought great
miracles both in ancient and in modern times is still abundantly available to us today. The Lord still tells us that
"according to men's faith it shall be done unto them."
All of us can have great blessings if we will but believe

with our whole hearts and souls and allow faith to operate in our lives.

What is the nature of this remarkable power? How can we make faith a fundamental part of our lives? Faith, as the term is used throughout the scriptures, implies "full confidence and trust in the being, purposes, and words of God."[1] When such confidence or trust is possessed by any individual, all doubt disappears. Such absolute confidence in God and in his promises leads naturally to the thoughts, actions, and convictions that will bring into being the thing in which one has faith.

Faith as a motivating spiritual power is a gift from God and must be God-centered rather than self-centered. This type of faith causes us to seek to do the will of the Lord rather than to concentrate on that which he can do for us. Instead of thinking of faith as a formula merely to get the Lord to do our bidding, we must try to find out what the Lord wants us to do and seek to pattern our lives according to his plan.

On one occasion, the Savior told his disciples that they should have faith as little children if they would be great in the kingdom of heaven. (Matt. 18:1-4.) We can all learn much from the simple faith of little children.

Recently a three-year-old girl lay apparently dying of a seemingly incurable disease. Looking up trustingly into the eyes of her grandmother she said, "Tell me the story of Jesus again, how he loved little children. Jesus is going to make me well." And because of her simple and complete faith and the faith of those who loved her most, she is today growing in health and strength.

If we feel that our faith is not as strong as we would like it to be, let us strengthen it by exercising it every day. Let us have faith in the ability of our children and help them constructively to develop their talents. Let us have faith in the goodness and kindness of our neighbors. In this way we will build our own characters and will concentrate on seeing only the good in others. Above all, let us have complete faith in our Father in heaven and in his desire to lead and guide us.

Let us always remember that faith "maketh an anchor to the souls of men, which . . . make them sure and steadfast. . . ." (Ether 12:4.)

---

[1]James E. Talmage, *Articles of Faith* (Salt Lake City: Church of Jesus Christ of Latter-day Saints, 1949), p. 96.

"Therefore, Ask
In Faith"

*Remember that without faith you can do
nothing; therefore ask in faith. Trifle not
with these things; do not ask for that which
you ought not.* (D&C 8:10.)

Faith is the motivating force of
action. It is the cornerstone of all religion, and the first
principle of the gospel of Jesus Christ.

The message of this important principle, as found in
the Doctrine and Covenants, Section 8, presents two areas
of thought. First, we are reminded that nothing can be ac-
complished without faith, be it great or small, miraculous
or commonplace. No work ever succeeded that was not
backed by faith. It is the essence of courage, strength, confidence, and trust.

Faith has been defined as "belief in action." All
around us we see faith in process. We see it in our every-
day activities of work and play. It is evident in the simple
activity of planting seeds with confidence that they will
sprout and grow to maturity.

Faith is solidly behind all of man's accomplishments,
whether they be great or small.

An effective vaccine has been developed that promises

to control the scourge of polio. This wonderful benefit to mankind came after years of painstaking labor and research, every step of which was founded on faith that a vaccine could be found.

The Lord achieves his divine purposes here upon the earth through the faith of mankind. He "workest unto the children of men according to their faith." (Ether 12:29.) He has promised, "Ask, and it shall be given you; seek, and ye shall find; knock, and it shall be opened unto you." (Matt. 7:7.) But, he also adds, ". . . let him ask in faith, nothing wavering. . . ." (James 1:6.)

The second area of the message indicates that one should not attempt to employ faith in the furthering of one's own selfish interests. The story is told of a young girl blessed with a great talent who won high honors in a national contest. When her grandfather congratulated her, she explained humbly that she had fasted and prayed and knew that the Lord would help her succeed. Her grandfather remarked that it was probable that the other contestants had prayed that they also might win. Whereupon the granddaughter replied, "I did not pray to win, but asked the Lord to help me to do my best. He helped me do my best, and even if I had not won the contest, still I would feel that I had succeeded."

It is a mark of sincere faith to ask the Lord to help us always to do our best. With this type of motivation we can move confidently forward to the full utilization of all of our talents and abilities and with full confidence of the Lord's blessings, for "whatsoever thing ye shall ask the Father in my name, which is good, in faith believing that ye shall receive, behold, it shall be done unto you." (Moroni 7:26.)

Faith is a gift from God. As with all other gifts, the more one exercises it, in a righteous way, the more it grows and develops. Finally it becomes a great motivating spiritual power in the lives of men. And to him who has such faith Jesus has promised, "nothing shall be impossible to you." (Matt. 17:20.)

Cease To
Find Fault

. . . cease to find fault one with another. . . .
(D&C 88:124.)

ONE of the most noble accomplish-
ments in this world is to exercise a constructive, uplifting
influence upon others. To touch a soul and to encourage
that soul to reach for loftier heights is far more important
than to build monuments of stone or steel.

No one of us is without influence. All of us touch the
lives of those about us for good or for ill. If we concentrate
upon and emphasize the good qualities that others possess,
we not only enlarge and ennoble our own character, but
we also help our neighbors to live upward and outward
and to develop the best that is within them.

On the other hand, if we seek to find fault, we soon
find that our own personalities become warped. Our criticism,
moreover, has a downgrading effect upon the person with
whom we have found fault.

In speaking of faultfinding, President McKay has said
that each of us should perform his duty honestly and conscientiously. We should not interfere with another who is

doing something in a different way. When we spend our time finding fault with others, we neglect our own responsibilities and our souls become embittered, our minds distorted, our judgments faulty, and our spirits depressed.[1]

That is why the Lord has commanded us to "cease to find fault one with another." That is why the wise Solomon, in describing seven things that the Lord hates, pointed out that five of the seven are directly connected with fault-finding.

Our Father in heaven has placed great emphasis on the value of a soul. He knows the potential that lies within us. He knows that, as his sons and daughters, we may become perfect, even as he is perfect, if we concentrate on and magnify the fine qualities that each of us possesses. To do this, we should form the habit of looking only for the good qualities in those with whom we associate, rather than seeing all their faults. It is easy for us to slip into the error of faultfinding. Often in attempting to cover up our own weaknesses, we may try to justify or rationalize them by looking for the same faults in others. This thought is expressed in the anonymous poem that has become a Latter-day Saint hymn:

> Let each man learn to know himself;
> To gain that knowledge let him labor,
> Improve those failings in himself
> Which he condemns so in his neighbor.
> How lenient our own faults we view,
> And conscience's voice adeptly smother,
> Yet, oh, how harshly we review
> The selfsame failings in another!
> Example sheds a genial ray
> Of light which men are apt to borrow,
> So first improve yourself today
> And then improve your friends tomorrow.[2]

The story is told about a church edifice in Germany that is famous for its beautiful stained-glass windows.

These windows, when viewed with the clear rays of the sun shining through them, are marvelous indeed. Many people are touched by their beauty. Yet many other visitors who do not take the time to look at the windows from the right angle, or who see them on a dark and foggy day, are disillusioned and dissatisfied. They see nothing to admire and only find fault with the church building.

So it is with many of us. In evaluating our friends' and neighbors' personalities and characters, we fail to view their accomplishments in the sunlight and glow of charity. We do not take the time and patience to look into their hearts. We let our vision of them become clouded and dimmed through misunderstanding.

Elder John A. Widtsoe, an apostle to the Lord Jesus Christ, once said:

> Faultfinding is dangerous. It grows easily into a habit; then spreads as a disease into every thought and act. It drives away cheer and banishes happiness. There are faults in every man. . . . Look for them and they are found. There are virtues in every man. Look for them and they are found. To dwell upon faults breeds distrust and illwill; to consider virtues creates confidence and begets love. . . .
>
> Whoever walks with the faults of the world, travels in darkness. . . . Whoever seeks the virtues of the world, lives in the light of day. . . . Expect perfection in no man.[3]

Let us "cease to find fault one with another" and look only for the good in others. Let us realize that often the mistakes of another might have been our own had we been influenced by similar circumstances.

Let us oft speak kind words to and of each other. Let us seek to build up one another, to give encouragement and appreciation when it is due. Let us always remember the words of the Lord when he said, "Give, and it shall be given unto you; good measure, pressed down, and shaken together, and running over. . . . For with the same measure

that ye mete withal it shall be measured to you again."
(Luke 6:38.)

---

[1]David O McKay, *Pathways to Happiness*, compiled by Llewellyn R. McKay (Salt Lake City: Bookcraft, 1956), p. 86.

[2]*Hymns*, No. 91.

[3]*The Improvement Era*, reprinted with permission from Leah D. Widstoe.

The Nobility
Of Forgiveness

Wherefore, I say unto you, that ye ought to forgive one another. . . . (D&C 64:9.)

THE PRINCIPLE of forgiveness, as described in this passage from the Doctrine and Covenants, is emphasized not only as a fundamental part of the gospel, but also as an essential guide to full, happy living. In Section 64 of the Doctrine and Covenants, the Lord gives the above quoted passage and then continues, ". . . for he that forgiveth not his brother his trespasses standeth condemned before the Lord; for there remaineth in him the greater sin." (D&C 64:9.) In other words, he who fails to forgive commits an even "greater sin" than he who has sinned against him.

Without doubt, the greatest example of divine forgiveness in the world was expressed in the dramatic words uttered by the Savior as he hung in agony on the cross: "Father, forgive them; for they know not what they do." (Luke 23:34.)

One of the glorious aspects of the principle of forgiveness is the purifying and ennobling effect its application has upon the personality and character of the forgiver.

Someone wisely said, "He who has not forgiven a wrong or an injury has not yet tasted one of the sublime enjoyments of life." The human soul seldom rises to such heights of strength and nobility as when it removes all resentments and forgives errors and malice.

When one harbors resentment against another, it does the recipient little harm, but it shrivels and corrodes the soul of the one holding the grudge. When one hates another for some real or imagined wrong, the feeling of hatred assumes power and dominion over one's thoughts, sleep, health, happiness, and even over one's appearance. The most expensive clothes and best beauty treatment cannot blot out the hard looks and appearance that are the by-products of hatred, resentment, and the unforgiving soul. Shakespeare said it this way: "Heat not a furnace for your foe so hot that it do singe yourself."

Jesus fully realized the damaging effect of unforgiveness upon our characters and personalities. He said, "Love your enemies, bless them that curse you, do good to them that hate you, and pray for them which despitefully use you, and persecute you." (Matt. 5:44.) This formula, if followed, will heal a troubled soul and enrich a personality.

One of the world's most beautiful mountains, located in Jasper National Park in Canada, was named for Edith Cavell. Edith Cavell was a war-time nurse executed by her enemies for having hidden, nursed, and fed wounded soldiers. As she stood before the firing squad she uttered these deathless words, now preserved in bronze and granite: "I realize that patriotism is not enough. I must have no hatred or bitterness toward anyone."

If we have been wronged or injured, forgiveness means to blot it completely from our minds. To forgive and forget is an ageless counsel. "To be wronged or robbed," said the Chinese philosopher Confucius, "is nothing unless you continue to remember it."

In addition to the purifying and ennobling effects forgiveness has upon our own souls, this principle comes to us as divine instruction from our Father in heaven and is a requisite upon which he grants us his forgiveness. It has been said, "He that cannot forgive others, breaks the bridge over which he must pass himself, for every man hath need to be forgiven." The Savior said, "For if ye forgive men their trespasses, your Heavenly Father will also forgive you." (Matt. 6:14.)

The Gift
Of Free Agency

Wherefore, hear my voice, follow me, and
you shall be a free people. . . . (D&C 38:22.)

Freedom and free agency are cornerstones of the foundation of the gospel and the plan of salvation. It is a divine truth that regardless of the shackles men try to impose upon themselves and upon each other, our Father in heaven's plan for his children is one of free agency. This thought is expressed in this well-known verse:

> *Know this, that every soul is free,*
> *To choose his life and what he'll be,*
> *For this eternal truth is given:*
> *That God will force no man to heaven.*[1]

Next to life itself, freedom is the most precious gift that God has given to man. It was bestowed upon us before the formation of this world. When the devil sought to destroy man's free agency, a great council was called in heaven, and Lucifer and his followers were cast out. The Savior's plan of free agency was adopted as the gospel plan of salvation that would guide and redeem mankind here upon the earth.[2]

Christ came to this earth and gave his life that we might be a free people. Lehi, the first Book of Mormon prophet, tells us that "the Messiah cometh in the fulness of time, that he may redeem the children of men. . . . And because that they are redeemed . . . they have become free forever, knowing good from evil; to act for themselves. . . ." (2 Nephi 2:26.)

President David O. McKay has said, "Next to the bestowal of life itself, the right to direct that life is God's greatest gift to man. . . . man's success or failure, happiness or misery depends upon what he seeks and what he chooses."[3]

An apostle of our church went behind the iron curtain in East Germany to hold a conference with the members of the Church there. Hundreds came to the meeting at great sacrifice and at considerable personal danger. After a spiritual feast together, these Saints returned willingly to their homes, although they live under the tyrannical oppression of a Communist regime.

Some of these members, who have relatively few family ties, might easily, as so many others are doing daily, have escaped into the bright sunlight of the free world. Yet, because of their love for spiritual freedom, these members returned to their homes where they can continue their efforts to keep the light of this spark from being completely extinguished. These members believe with the apostle Paul: ". . . where the spirit of the Lord is, there is liberty." (2 Cor. 3:17.)

This Doctrine and Covenants truth, "Wherefore hear my voice, follow me, and you shall be a free people," emphasizes the freedom that comes from listening to and following the Savior's teachings. He has promised that if we learn his laws and commandments and apply them to our lives, we will be a free people. We must, however, seek continuously for a knowledge of his truths. The Savior himself declared, ". . . ye shall know the truth, and the truth shall make you free." (John 8:32.)

As we seek to preserve our freedom, we should be alert to another type of bondage that can enslave us. This bondage we impose upon ourselves through harmful habits and negative and destructive thinking. This self-inflicted bondage can remove our freedom more effectively than even the slavery imposed by tyrants. The only way we can keep from falling into this type of bondage is to accept the Savior's counsel and follow his teachings.

Both by precept and example the Savior has shown us how to keep love in our hearts and how to keep ourselves from destructive thoughts and influences.

Someone has wisely said, "Freedom is not free. If we want to keep it, we need to love it, live it, work for it, even fight for it."

---

[1]William C. Gregg, *Hymns*, No. 90.
[2]See Rev. 12:7-9; D&C 29:36-39; Moses 4:1, 4.
[3]*Pathways to Happiness*, compiled by Llewellyn R. McKay (Salt Lake City: Bookcraft, 1957).

Freedom Through Righteous Living

*Abide ye in the liberty wherewith ye are
made free; entangle not yourselves in sin. . . .*
(D&C 88:86.)

THE COMPLETE passage in the Doctrine and Covenants from which the above statement is taken reads "Abide ye in the liberty wherewith ye are made free; entangle not yourselves in sin, but let your hands be clean, until the Lord comes."

The emphasis in this inspired scripture is on the unalterable fact that righteous living blesses the human soul with freedom. On the other hand, the entanglement of sin brings bondage. All of life's experiences prove the truthfulness of these statements.

Sin, as the apostle John pointed out, "is the transgression of the law." (1 John 3:4.) Laws are established to ensure man's freedom. This is true in both secular and spiritual laws.

In a free country police forces are established so that men may move freely in their communities without fear of molestation or danger to their lives or personal property. Likewise, God's laws are established to guarantee our freedom.

The Ten Commandments were given not as restraints or impositions, but rather as guides to full and purposeful living. Man cannot break God's commandments nor the laws of nature; rather, if he attempts to violate them, he breaks himself against them and destroys his personal freedom. The Lord has said, "I, the Lord God, make you free, therefore ye are free indeed; and the law also maketh you free." (D&C 98:8.)

Elder Hugh B. Brown tells the story of the skilled airplane manufacturer who perfected the design for a special aircraft. He invented and fitted together all the operating parts into a mechanical symphony. Then he turned the plane over to his son, the pilot, with the caution that the success or failure of the aircraft would depend upon how carefully he observed the laws upon which the flight depended. The builder outlined to his son the steps he must take in preparation for each flight and exactly what he could do and could not do as he met certain types of flying conditions. These he gave to his son as "Thou shalt" and "Thou shalt not."

At first the son followed his father's instructions explicitly. But soon he felt the thrill of the release of restraint and began to take chances based on freedoms of his own decisions. Under these conditions it was not long until the pilot encountered flying circumstances that even this remarkable machine could not handle, and the inevitable tragic crash resulted.

After recounting this incident, President Brown concludes: "Every man is the pilot of his own life, charged with the responsibility of flight across the valley of life and over the hills of eternity. We must keep in mind that the Creator is our Father and heed his warnings, for his purpose is to help us make a perfect landing."[1]

If we really desire to maintain our God-given freedom under his divine plan of free agency, we must free ourselves from the pitfalls of sin and from the transgression of the law. Let us keep from being led into temptation. Let us seek those experiences that will help us develop the most worthwhile qualities of our characters and personalities.

Let us seek wholesome companionships and environments and search for the good and beautiful in life. In all of our actions, let us scrupulously avoid compromising with truth and honesty. We should strive to think pure, wholesome thoughts, for, "as he thinketh in his heart, so is he." (Prov. 23:7.)

Safety and freedom lie in resisting temptation and avoiding even the appearance of evil, and in living and applying those virtues as exemplified in the life of our Savior, Jesus Christ.

This excerpt from Alexander Pope's "Essay on Man" beautifully expresses the dangers of associating with sin:

Sin is a monster of so frightful mien,
As to be hated needs but to be seen;
Yet seen too oft, familiar with her face,
We first endure, then pity, then embrace.

If we abide in the liberty of righteous living, though we be shackled in chains, still we will be free. True freedom comes from within, for our spirits are free from the burdens of a guilty conscience.

If we know we are in the right, we have the rich fruits of freedom, among which are tranquility and peace of mind. These are among the freedoms that the Savior's life taught and exemplified. He said, "Peace I leave with you, my peace I give unto you: not as the world giveth, give I unto you. Let not your heart be troubled, neither let it be afraid." (John 14:27.)

---

[1]Hugh B. Brown, *Eternal Quest* (Salt Lake City: Bookcraft), p. 297.

Divine Gifts

. . . every man is given a gift by the Spirit of God . . . that all may be profited thereby. (D&C 47:11-12.)

A⊤ THE Christmas season, when our thoughts are centered on gifts and giving, how often do we pause to consider the countless wonderful gifts that our Father in heaven has so lovingly bestowed upon each of us? We believe that the greatest gifts ever given to man are the gift of free agency and the gift of the atoning sacrifice of our Savior, whose birth we celebrate at Christmastime and whose spirit should motivate all of our thoughts and actions. But along with these great gifts, the Lord has bestowed bounteous individual gifts and talents upon each of us.

The important challenge we all face is to recognize the gifts and talents we possess and to develop them to the maximum, not only for our own benefit, but also for the benefit of others. What are these gifts? How can we develop and utilize them to the best advantage?

When we speak of the gifts of God, often we are inclined to think only of spiritual gifts, such as the gifts

of faith and of healing. These, of course, are blessed
special gifts, but the Lord has bestowed other gifts upon
us that are also wonderful. For example, Brigham Young
once said, "The gift of communicating one with another
is the gift of God, just as much as the gift of prophecy."[1]
Likewise, the gift of an understanding heart, of a desire
to serve, of cheerfulness, the ability to teach, the wonderful character trait of looking for and magnifying the good
in others—all these are gifts from God. These are gifts
that we all can possess if we seek diligently to develop
them.

The words "gifts" and "talents" are often employed
synonymously. These words have been defined as "natural
endowments employing favor by God and given to us as a
divine trust."

Far too many of us fail to recognize the many wonderful talents and gifts with which we are endowed. We
look at some of our friends and acquaintances who seem
to be talented and wish we possessed similar accomplishments. Unfortunately, some of us make the mistake of
trying to imitate these talents rather than to search out
and develop those with which we ourselves have been
blessed. Actually, as the scripture states, the Lord gives
many gifts but "to some is given one and to some is given
another," in order that through the wise development of
these gifts "all may be profited thereby."

All of us have gifts that are distinctly our own.
It is our individual responsibility and opportunity to discover, develop, and use these priceless gifts.

One of the best known stories that emphasizes the
importance of discovering and using our gifts or talents
wisely is contained in the parable told by Jesus: "For the
kingdom of heaven is as a man travelling into a far country who called his own servants, and delivered unto them
his goods.

"And unto one he gave five talents, to another two,

and to another one; to every man according to his several ability; and straightway took his journey."

The story continues with the description of how two servants used their talents productively and expanded and multiplied them. The third servant buried his talents in the ground, with the result that when the master returned, even that little which had been given to him was taken away. (See Matt. 25:14-29.)

This parable dramatizes with clarity the important fact that unless we develop and use the gifts we have been given, we will lose them. As underscored in the Doctrine and Covenants scripture, these talents must be used freely and joyously for the good of all mankind. One wise man has said, "No man has come to true greatness who has not felt in some degree that his life belongs to his race, and that what God gives him he gives him for mankind."[2]

As we develop our talents unselfishly for the good of all, we recognize the universal truth that "it is more blessed to give than to receive."

The real spirit of Christmas is the spirit of service to others. In all our giving let us remember that the most precious gifts are those centered in love, in thoughtfulness, kindness, and other gifts from the heart. Although such gifts cannot be wrapped in gay paper and tied with tinsel cord, they will outlast those that human hands can create and will bring to us deeper joy than all the riches of the world. With these gifts we can extend the spirit of Christmas throughout the year and throughout our lives and can thus develop those gifts and talents that God so generously bestowed upon us.

---

[1]Brigham Young, *Journal of Discourses*, Vol. 3, p. 364 (June 22, 1856).
[2]Phillip Brooks, in *Useful Quotations* (Grosset & Dunlap, 1933), p. 234.

The Lord's
Gifts Accepted

*For what doth it profit a man if a gift is
bestowed upon him, and he receive not the
gift?* (D&C 88:33)

EACH of us is endowed with cer-
tain gifts from our Father in heaven. These gifts are given
to us individually and personally so that we may, if we receive and magnify them, reach to greater heights in the
development of our personalities, our characters, and our
abilities.

The Lord tells us in the Doctrine and Covenants,
". . . to every man is given a gift by the Spirit of God. To
some is given one, and to some is given another, that all
may be profited thereby." (D&C 46:11-12.) Whether or not
we enjoy these gifts and thus reach the heights the Lord
expects of us depends upon our willingness and worthiness
to accept them. "For what doth it profit a man if a gift
is bestowed upon him, and he receive not the gift?"

We must remember that these gifts are from a loving
Father in heaven who wants us to be happy and to succeed
in life. Yet, they are given to us on the promise that they
will be ours only if we accept and magnify them. If we

fail to receive and develop them in the way that we should, they will be taken away from us. The Prophet Joseph Smith said:

> *Blessings offered, but rejected, are no longer blessings . . . the proffered good returns to the giver; the blessing is bestowed on those who will receive and occupy; for unto him that hath shall be given, and he shall have abundantly, but unto him that hath not or will not receive, shall be taken away that which he hath, or might have had.*[1]

How can we develop most effectively the gifts that have been bestowed upon us? Certainly one approach would be for us to recognize the gifts or potentials that lie within us, desire to develop them, have the faith that we can develop them, and then go about confidently practicing and applying the actions that will magnify and develop them. The apostle Paul said, "Neglect not the gift that is in thee. . . . give thyself wholly to them; that thy profiting may appear to all." (1 Tim. 4:14-15.)

We often refer to the wisdom of Solomon. In so doing we may wish that we might possess this great wisdom. If we really desire to develop the gift of wisdom, we must practice those qualities which will help us to become wise. For example, before we make any important decisions with respect to any problem, we should get all possible facts and then make sure we evaluate. If we desire the great gift of knowledge, we must be willing to study and yearn for learning. If we desire to develop the wondrous gift of faith, this can be obtained only if we practice believing and following the Lord's commandments.

We have been admonished to seek "earnestly the best gifts, always remembering for what they are given; For verily I say unto you, they are given for the benefit of those who love me and keep all my commandments. . . ." (D&C 46:8-9.)

A young man was overheard complaining that he had no talents and implying that when God had distributed gifts, he had been passed by. This young man, in fact, seemed proud of his modesty and apparent humility in recognizing his own inadequacies. Actually, he possessed a substantial potential that he was wasting by his negative attitude toward himself and by refusing to recognize his inherent capabilities. In an effort to help him, a wise counselor suggested that he select one simple gift that he definitely possessed. This was a special ability to be friendly. He was encouraged to appreciate and to exercise faith in this one gift and then earnestly work to magnify it. In so doing, he soon found he had other gifts that had been lying dormant. By concentrating on each gift and seeking to magnify it, he succeeded in raising all of his talents and abilities to a higher level of performance.

Someone has observed that when we develop one trait fully, there is a tendency for that one trait to pull all the others up to its stature. President Joseph F. Smith has said, "Every son and every daughter of God has received some talent [or gift], and each will be held to strict account for the use or misuse to which it is put."[2]

The Lord has many gifts for each of us if we have the faith, courage, willpower, and fortitude to work for them. The Lord can and wants to give them to us, but they can become ours only if we accept and use them. "For what doth it profit a man if a gift is bestowed upon him, and he receive not the gift? Behold, he rejoices not in that which is given unto him, neither rejoices in him who is the giver of the gift."

---

[1]*History of the Church,* Vol. 5, p. 135.
[2]*Juvenile Instructor,* Vol. 38 (1903), p. 689.

Seek
Divine Guidance

. . . seek not to counsel your God.
(D&C 22:4.)

T HE idea that any of us might ever seek to advise or counsel our Father in heaven would seem, on first thought, to be incredible. Only the most rebellious among us, it would appear, would ever resort to such action. However, the truth is that on occasion all of us, often unknowingly, have sought to counsel the Lord. We are guilty of this attempted action if, for example, in our prayers we seek to instruct our Father in heaven in the way we expect him to fulfill our requests, rather than to petition him humbly for guidance and help.

We also fall into the error of seeking to counsel the Lord if, at any time, we attempt to interpret the Lord's teachings so that they fit our own particular interests and desires. Sometimes when we fail to understand a principle of the gospel, or are not fully in accord with it, we seek to counsel God by minimizing the importance of the principle. We might even attempt to alter the meaning of the Lord's word in our minds to suit our own convenience and purpose.

The essence of full compliance with the Lord's counsel is to be obedient to all his laws and commandments as he has given them and as they have been interpreted by his prophets. We should not seek to find ways to circumvent his teachings and interpret them according to our own desires. Elder Marion G. Romney emphasized this point in an address at a general church conference when he said: "We ought to obey the Lord's commandments as they are given. We ought not to twist and turn and bend them to our will."

Sometimes, when we are faced with life's pressing problems, unconsciously we counsel the Lord by asking him to solve our problems in a certain way.

A few years ago a fine Latter-day Saint woman was facing a crisis in her life. In her limited knowledge she could see only one solution to her problem. She prayed earnestly to the Lord for that particular solution. One night when she couldn't sleep she opened the Book of Mormon to Jacob 4:10:

> . . . seek not to counsel the Lord, but to take counsel from his hand. For . . . he counseleth in wisdom, and in justice, and in great mercy, over all his works.

She slipped out of bed and humbly asked forgiveness of the Lord for the way she had prayed previously. She then proceeded to pray for guidance in the solution of her problem, yielding herself completely to God's will. For the first time in months a peace came into her soul. Her problem was never solved in the way she originally wanted, but she knew the Lord's solution was the right one. A year or two later she could see clearly the wisdom of the Lord's answer to her problem.

We all need to search our souls and make sure we do not fall into the error of seeking to counsel the Lord. When we pray to our Heavenly Father, we should approach him in humility and in obedience, with complete faith and trust in his all-seeing wisdom.

We should seek the Lord's counsel in all things with the full assurance that he knows what is best for us. We should have uppermost in our hearts the thought, "Teach me thy way, O Lord . . ." (Ps. 27:11), rather than "let me have" my way. We must remember that the Lord is our ever-loving Father in heaven who is interested in our well-being. He knows the full purpose of our lives and can see the beginning and the end. If we are faithful and prayerful and submit ourselves to his will, he will direct our paths for good.

Jesus, the supreme model, gave us the true approach. Although he possessed all knowledge and wisdom, still he prayed constantly to his Father in heaven, acknowledging his Father's superiority in all things. Christ's very life exemplified his meaningful words when he said to his Father, ". . . not my will, but thine, be done." (Luke 22:42.)

Spiritual Beauty
In The Home

THROUGHOUT the teachings contained in the Doctrine and Covenants, great emphasis is placed upon the responsibilities of parents to rear their children in the ways of righteousness and to teach them the importance of harmony, unity, prayerfulness, and kindness.

Some of the Doctrine and Covenants' passages that emphasize these teachings are as follows:

> *And they shall also teach their children to pray, and to walk uprightly before the Lord.* (D&C 68:28.)
>
> *. . . bring up your children in light and truth.* (D&C 93:40.)
>
> *Thou shalt live together in love. . . .* (D&C 42:45.)
>
> *Remember faith, virtue, knowledge, temperance, patience, brotherly kindness, godliness, charity, humility, diligence.* (D&C 4:6.)

Beauty in the home comes from much more than just physical surroundings. It exists where there are love, understanding, unity, kindness, and an atmosphere of peace and serenity.

Recently a national magazine featured an unusual family that lives in an unusual place. This family makes its home at the bottom of a steep canyon on the winding Snake River. Here, without many of the common household conveniences, these parents have reared eleven children. We are told that theirs is a happier, more satisfying life than that of most conventional householders. In this secluded canyon, the parents and children depend upon each other for companionship and upon a colorful wilderness for enjoyment and recreation. One of the children remarked, "As for television, who needs that when one lives in an enchanted canyon?"

Few people could or would want to live in an isolated canyon. Yet, it is impressive that without many of the physical home conveniences, which we feel are so necessary to our own happiness, this family, apparently, has built much beauty into its home.

All of us strive to make our homes places of beauty. Many of us search long and hard to find just the right piece of furniture, the right accessories and color scheme, to achieve this beauty. Surely the physical beauty of a home is important to our comfort and well-being.

Still, another type of beauty is far more essential. This beauty is an atmosphere, a climate, the spirit of the home, the attitude of its inhabitants one toward the other. At first glance these may seem intangibles, but actually they are as real and as accessible as the smile on a face, the friendly light in one's eyes, the kind words on lips, and the expression of love and understanding in hearts. This is the type of beauty that one may not be able to touch or to describe, but it can be felt and sensed the very moment one enters a home.

This type of beauty is well within the reach of everyone. It can be found in the humblest cottage, in the tiniest apartment, as well as in a palatial home. And, as with most great things in life, it is free for the asking. We can buy palatial homes and extravagant furnishings, but we cannot give silver or gold for peace or happiness. We can pay for pleasures and luxuries, but we cannot buy love.

Many are prone to think of beauty only in its objective, physical state. Yet the wise men of the ages, who have attempted to define and analyse beauty, all agree that its spiritual aspects are of paramount importance. Socrates, Aristotle, Plato, and Aquinas all describe beauty as synonymous with truth, goodness, harmony, unity, and tranquility. These are values well within the reach of everyone. Through their application, we can bring a feeling of serenity, peace, and rest into our homes. In a home where this type of beauty is present, jealousy, fear, and insecurity are banished and replaced with settled courage, faith, and trust.

As we think back into the early experiences in our own home life, what are the pleasant things that come first to mind? Are they the big things associated with material possessions, or are they the simple, little, heart-warming things, such as the fragrance of newly baked bread, the feeling of "togetherness" as the family met daily around the dining table, the spiritual uplift of family prayers, the memory of loving friends stopping in for a chat and a piece of grandmother's wonderful apple pie?

Do we remember the little acts of thoughtfulness and kindness our mother performed each day—the smile on her face, and the fact that she was always there to mend a bruised knee or a broken heart? Today, in our busy schedules, are we providing these types of surroundings and these memories for our children? These are the so-called intangible qualities that are so important, if we would have real and lasting beauty in our homes.

All of us need beauty to make our lives complete. And we all have that beauty within us, though we express it in different ways. The poet expresses it in words; the artist uses canvas and colors; the sculptor, stone. The mother expresses it in the tender love for her child. Each one of us in our every-day contact with one another can express the beauty within us. We can mingle with one another in a spirit of consideration and thoughtfulness. We can be gentle, patient, and courteous. We can govern our actions with a kindly regard for others. We can radiate cheerfulness wherever we go. For cheerfulness is also an expression of beauty, and it will reflect in the attitude of everyone we meet, just as surely as a beautiful flower drooping over the edge of a pond reflects in the water.

A young mother told how her six-year-old daughter brought her back abruptly to reality and the importance of cheerfulness. It was one of those busy, frustrating mornings, and this mother was hurrying through her work with what must have been a grim expression on her face, when she noticed her daughter looking at her intently. Finally the little girl said: "I was just thinking, mama, how pretty your face is when you smile."

In the home where spiritual beauty is stressed, we will find kindness, for kindness dwells in each member's heart. We will find good-humored tolerance of others, because forgiveness is practiced. In this type of home, courtesy for one another will abound, for each member has formed the habit of being kind, loving, and patient.

The story is told of a wise grandmother who was also a fine cook. She brought many choice recipes with her from the "old country." One day she was sharing a recipe with a friend; after telling her to take so many cups of this and tablespoons of that, the grandmother finished with, "But remember, Carrie, if the soup is to be a success, you must also add a generous amount of grace."

To a young granddaughter who was listening to the conversation, this seemed very strange. She hadn't seen any cans on the cupboard shelves marked "grace," and she told her grandmother so. The grandmother thoughtfully replied, "My dear, no matter what you do in life, whether it's making Danish soup, singing a lullaby, or writing a book, if you would know the true flavor of living, you must give generously of yourself, of your sweet spirit, of your love. You must add grace."

Each of us should strive to add the important ingredient of "grace" to our lives. Let us always remember that lasting, permanent beauty in our hearts and in our homes is made up of encouraging words, loving deeds, sympathy expressed, heartaches healed, a kiss, a smile, a song that makes us feel light-hearted, free, and glad.

These are tried links that, when bound together, make a golden chain of beauty around our doors. Such beauty, if practiced, will shine out in our souls as well as in our homes.

The True
Meaning Of
Honesty

And let every man deal honestly. . . .
(D&C 51:9.)

W HAT an ideal place this world
would be if all men followed the commandment, as found
in D&C 51:9, and dealt honestly one with another. If each
individual and each nation could trust each other implicitly,
there would be no more wars or contention in the land.
Neighbors would live peaceably and amicably together,
for "one who is honest . . . is always disposed to act with
careful regard for the rights of others, and will do nothing
unworthy of his own inherent nobility of soul."[1]

Honesty is the essence of individual good character.
It is also one of the solid rocks upon which civilization has
been built. Honest people, who sustain the law and deal
justly one with another, constitute the pillars of our civil-
ized society. Such individuals adhere rigidly to the truth.
No one questions their integrity! They are, in fact, as
Alexander Pope said, "The noblest work of God."

Most conscientious individuals think of themselves
as being honest, and if their honesty were questioned they

would be offended. Why, then, has the Lord given us this commandment? Is dishonesty a character weakness limited only to the so-called wicked?

Certainly the general over-all pattern of our lives is built around honesty. However, when we examine all the different facets of the word, we begin to realize that strict and complete honesty is difficult to practice. Diogenes, a well-known Greek philosopher, maintained that a strictly honest person was impossible to find, and to illustrate his conviction, it was said that "he went about the streets of Corinth in broad daylight with a lighted lantern looking for an honest man."

Most of us exhibit honesty in our dealings with the big things in life. It is in the seeming trifles of daily living that our honesty is most seriously challenged. For example, these seeming trifles include the little untruths that at the moment seem unimportant, exaggerations that make things appear different than they really are, little breaches of the law, stretching the truth when it seems convenient to do so. These are the types of seemingly unimportant dishonesties into which it is so easy for us to fall. Yet, we should remember, as someone has so wisely said, "There is no such thing as a little dishonesty."

Honesty, like most virtues, is best learned at home. Parents must live honest lives if they want their children to live uprightly. Someone has said, "When a child who is punished for lying hears his parents successfully use a lie to evade a social commitment, he can only deduce that he was punished not for lying but for doing so ineptly; his resolve, then, is not always to tell the truth, but to perfect himself in the art of lying."

Often a child will put pressure on his parents to do something the parents and the child know to be wrong, such as driving the family car before legal age or signing a statement saying the child has completed successfully an assigned task at home, when the task has not been done.

The strictly honest parent will never give in to such pressures, because he knows that by so doing the child is not only taught dishonesty by example, but also loses confidence in his parents. Shakespeare expressed this truth when he said: "No legacy is so rich as honesty." Are we leaving this legacy to our children?

Honesty, in its broadest sense, is more than just keeping the commandments, "Thou shalt not steal [and] Thou shalt not bear false witness." It embraces keeping our word and our promises. It means not coveting that which does not belong to us nor pretending to be that which we are not. Honesty involves putting our best self into our work, giving full service, and being strict in the fulfillment of all our engagements and obligations.

One of the encouraging aspects of this commandment regarding honesty is that all of us have a built-in detector, our conscience, which never fails unless it is allowed to become dulled. Providentially, our Father in heaven placed within the human soul a moral reactor that automatically tells us whether or not a thought or action is right.

The story is told of a young soldier stationed on a South Pacific island who wanted to trade some cheap gadgets for some beautifully carved ivory. When the trade was completed the native islander remarked, "Are you satisfied?"

"What do you mean?" asked the soldier.

The islander replied, "Years ago a missionary came to these islands. He taught us to be true to 'the man within.' I am wondering if you are fully satisfied?"

"No," said the soldier, "I am not satisfied. Here are the ivory and the gadgets. Take them both, and thank you for sharpening my conscience."

Since man's existence upon the earth, he has been exhorted both directly by the Lord and through his servants the prophets to walk uprightly and honestly. No principle of living is more important to our own joy and satisfaction and to the establishment of a lasting society.

---

[1]James C. Fernald, *Synonyms* (New York: Funk and Wagnalls, 1947), p. 239.

The Strength
Of Humility

And inasmuch as they were humble they might be made strong, and blessed from on high. . . . (D&C 1:28.)

As one studies the scriptures, he is impressed with the fact that great emphasis is placed upon the virtue of humility. True humility lies at the base of many of life's desirable virtues.

Godliness and the order of God's kingdom are predicated upon humility.

One cannot serve the Lord wholeheartedly unless he loses his selfish interests and conforms his individual will to the Lord's will, for our Father in heaven has said, ". . . no one can assist in this work except he shall be humble and full of love, having faith, hope, and charity. . . ." (D&C 12:8.) Neither can one obtain spiritual blessings unless he puts aside selfishness, self-dependence, pride, and arrogance. The Lord has declared:

> *. . . They who are puffed up because of their learning, and their wisdom, and their riches—yea, they are they whom he despiseth, and save they shall cast these things away, . . . and come down in the depths of humility, he will not open [the gates of heaven] unto them.* (2 Nephi 9:42.)

> *For whosoever exalteth himself shall be abased; and he that humbleth himself shall be exalted. (Luke 14:11.)*
>
> *Let him that is ignorant learn wisdom by humbling himself and calling upon the Lord. . . . For my spirit is sent forth into the world to enlighten the humble and contrite. . . . (D&C 136: 32-33.)*

Many years ago a religious leader was asked, "What is the first article of the Christian religion?" He answered, "Humility." Then he was asked, "What is the second?" He answered, "Humility." "And the third?" Again the leader answered, "Humility."

The need for humility is prominent in all of Jesus' teachings. As in all other things, Jesus himself set the perfect example. Although he was the "light and life of the world, the alpha and omega," the architect and builder of the universe, still he was born under the humblest of circumstances. His entire life was lived in a simple, modest way. He said repeatedly that his mission was to minister to the people, not to be ministered unto. He gave new glory and meaning to the word humility, for he declared himself to be "meek and lowly in heart." (Matt. 11:29.)

The following incident is probably the most classic example of true humility in all history.

> *. . . Jesus knew that his hour was come that he should depart out of this world, . . . knowing that the Father had given all things into his hands, and that he was come from God, and went to God; He riseth from supper, and laid aside his garments; and took a towel, and girded himself . . . and began to wash the disciples feet, and to wipe them with the towel wherewith he was girded. (John 13:1-5.)*

Yet, in all his humility Jesus never forgot his dignity. When Pilate asked him, "Art thou a king then?" Jesus answered, "Thou sayest that I am a king. To this end was I born. . . ." (John 18:37.)

Genuine humility leads the strong to serve the weak. It never underestimates its own worth. It does not infer in any way weakness, inadequacy, or self-abasement. Rather, true humility is a mark of genuine nobility. It is associated with courage, integrity, faith, and love. Those who possess it are teachable. "Whosoever shall humble himself as this little child, the same is greatest in the kingdom of heaven." (Matt. 18:4.)

Humility indicates a desire to serve. ". . . he that is greatest among you shall be your servant." (Matt. 23:11.)

Humility means that one recognizes dependence upon the Lord and soulfully expresses thankfulness for his great blessings.

Humility means being "meek and lowly in heart," charitable, and considerate of the rights and feelings of others. "Blessed are the meek: for they shall inherit the earth." (Matt. 5:5.)

Since the beginning of time, truly great leaders have been humble men and women. An outstanding example is that of Nephi, son of Lehi and founder of the Nephite nation, who "was one of the most lovable of men, true as steel, never wavering, full of integrity, faith and zeal; he loved the Lord with all his heart. . . . He was naturally a leader, his faith and courage made him so, while his devout humility gave him strength from heaven."[1]

Our latter-day prophets and leaders are humble individuals. They are powerful, for the spirit of the Lord is with them.

Strength springs from humility. Those who lay their souls bare, who recognize their weaknesses and banish vanity and pride from their hearts, put themselves in a position to receive the blessings and strength from their Father in heaven.

Humility is a noble virtue. Although it reflects itself in meekness, gentleness, and submissiveness to the Lord's will, yet it in no way implies self-depreciation or weakness. Humility is actually the foundation of strength. In order to gain moral and spiritual strength, one must first recognize his shortcomings and failings and then acknowledge his dependence upon the Lord. He must seek to do the Lord's will and have faith and trust in his guidance. Thus, with the Lord's help, he overcomes his weaknesses and replaces them with the virtues that bring strength.

Truly, those who are humble "are blessed from on high."

---

[1]George Reynolds, A *Dictionary of the Book of Mormon* (Salt Lake City: Joseph Hyrum Parry, 1891), p. 257.

The Meaning
Of Idleness

Thou shalt not be idle. . . . (D&C 42:42.)

IN THIS nuclear, automated, busy life, most of us would be shocked if we were accused of being idle. In our rush from task to task and from responsibility to responsibility, the majority of us can't seem to stretch our twenty-four-hour days far enough to accomplish all we wish to do.

Could this commandment, then, possibly apply to us today? Despite the rush of our lives, could we still be guilty of being idle? What is meant by being idle?

Socrates said, "Not only is he idle who is doing nothing, but he that might be better employed." The dictionary tells us that "idleness is not the absence of action; it denotes vain action. It is the absence of useful effective action."

Then the question we might ask ourselves is this: Are we avoiding idleness by using our time to the best advantage? If we are willing to accept this interpretation of the meaning of idleness, then, when we clutter our lives with futile, vain, or trifling activities, we are guilty of being idle. Likewise, if we allow our time to be consumed in aimless pursuits, if we do not improve ourselves, the situation of our neighbors, or the character of our environment, we are idle.

Fully aware of our human tendencies to "busy" ourselves with idleness, our Father in heaven, through his prophets over the ages, has repeatedly warned us to use our time constructively. We are told that "in the sweat of thy face shalt thou eat bread." (Gen. 3:19.) In these modern days, with the many complex demands upon our time, we again have been admonished to avoid idleness. We are told, "Thou shalt not be idle; for he that is idle shall not eat the bread nor wear the garments of the laborer." (D&C 43:42.)

In applying this commandment to our own lives, we must not overlook the fact that idleness has spiritual and mental as well as physical implications. Regardless of how busy we may be in a physical sense, many of us may actually be idle in developing ourselves mentally and spiritually. If we fail to use our time constructively, to develop ourselves mentally and spiritually, we are idle and cannot hope to "eat the bread or wear the garments of the laborer." The food that nourishes us spiritually and mentally we ourselves must prepare; no one else can do it for us.

In his epistle to Timothy, Paul chides the members of the Church for being idle. ". . . wandering about from house to house; and not only idle, but tattlers also and busybodies, speaking things which they ought not." (1 Tim. 5:13.) Ezekiel, in describing the sins and iniquity of Sodom, said, ". . . pride . . . abundance of idleness was in her and in her daughters, neither did she strengthen the hand of the poor and needy." (Ezek. 16:49.)

Even the most industrious of us must constantly be alert to the evil of idleness, for, like all insidious influences, idleness is a subtle thing. It can grow on us gradually,

unnoticed, unrecognized. Someone has said, "Idleness begins with fine cobwebs but ends in iron chains." Some of
us resist admitting this subtle growth, endeavoring to hide
or to justify our vain and trifling actions even to ourselves.
Finally, we find it is too late, and we are already enmeshed
in the bondage of futility.

The story is told of an individual who had a dream
about a large building where people attempted to buy
back precious time they had squandered.

First came a young man who said, "I have been promised an important position if I am prepared to take it.
But I am not prepared. The two years I should have spent
in study, I used in frivolous pastimes. Let me buy back
those two years of time."

Next in line was an older woman who said to the
clerk, "When it was too late, I discovered that God had
given me great talents that I failed to develop. Sell me
back ten years, that I might be the woman I could have
been."

How thankful we should be that the Lord has given
us twenty-four hours each day of precious time we can
use constructively to improve our lives and build solid
foundations for happiness.

With the gifts of life and free agency, we can, if
we so desire, organize our time so as to employ it advan-
tageously. In exercising our free agency in this modern day,
we should avoid cluttering our minds with shoddy literature. We should shun the wastefulness of trashy movies,
T.V. shows, and radio programs. Unless we are extremely
selective, these can consume our precious hours. These
wasteful activities can press in on us and make us think
we are busy when actually our time could be better used
for beautiful, useful, and soul-satisfying activities.

We should be deeply grateful for the wonderful opportunities of avoiding idleness through service in the Church.

In the wide variety of activities offered in the Church programs, we can develop our talents while serving.

Let us strive to place the right appraisal upon the values in life. Then shall we know the joys and satisfactions of a life free from idleness.

Eternal
Justice

*Leave judgment alone with me, for it is
mine and I will repay. . . . (D&C 82:23.)*

THE tendency to pass quick judg-
ment on others is one of the most common of our human
weaknesses. It is so easy to observe the actions of others
and to come to quick conclusions regarding their motives
and intentions. Consequently, all of us are prone to fall
into the error of quick, unqualified; and unjustified judgments.

This is a human frailty against which we have been
frequently warned and about which we should be constantly on guard. As the Lord says, we must leave judgment alone with him, for he alone can know the reasons
for human actions and what lies in the human heart.

President David O. McKay, in discussing our proneness to judge, told the story of a poor old Frenchwoman
who was walking along the banks of the Seine River.
"She had a threadbare shawl around her shoulders. She
stooped and picked up something and put it under her
shawl. A policeman a short distance away saw the act.

He hurried over to her and said, 'Let me see what you are holding under your shawl.'

"She drew out a piece of glass, saying, 'It is only a broken piece of glass. I picked it up because, perhaps, some barefoot boy might cut his foot on it.'

"What a lesson to the policeman who misjudged her! Yes, I know he was doing his duty, but he thought she was taking something which did not belong to her, when her act reflected the nobility of a great soul."[1]

What a lesson to all of us! How often in observing an action or an attitude on the part of one of our neighbors or friends have we been prone to impute motives and reasons that, because of our lack of full information, are wrong and misguided. Let us remember that in our limited knowledge, it is impossible for us to know the circumstances that prompt others' actions.

This poem, which has been put to music, stresses the challenge we face in really knowing one another:

> If I knew you and you knew me,
> If both of us could plainly see
> And understand with sight divine,
> The meaning of your heart and mine;
> And clasp our hands in friendliness;
> Our thoughts would pleasantly agree
> If I knew you and you knew me.
>
> I can't know you, you can't know me;
> The best in each we never see—
> The kindly thought, the hidden word,
> The melody that's never heard—
> But loving acts and deeds divine
> From human hearts may freely shine,
> And through them only may it be
> That I know you and you know me.
> —Anonymous

The Lord alone knows the capabilities, the thoughts, needs, and desires, that motivate human action. In the book of Psalms we read: ". . . he [the Lord] hath prepared his throne for judgment. And he shall judge the world in righteousness, he shall minister judgment to the people in uprightness." (Ps. 9:7-8.)

The Savior said, "Judge not, that ye be not judged." (Matt. 7:1.) The scriptures repeatedly emphasize that by the judgment we mete to others we also shall be judged.

The best way to overcome our proneness to judge others is to form the wonderful habit of looking for their good qualities rather than for their faults.

A certain individual had fallen into the habit of criticizing and complaining about an acquaintance with whom he was in close asssociation. In discussing the problem with a friend, he was asked, "Does not your associate have any good qualities?" To this he replied, "Yes, he is generous to a fault."

This appraisal started him thinking about the man's good qualities. Each time a negative or fault-finding thought entered his mind, he immediately tried to think of a good quality with which to replace it. As a consequence, this approach soon revealed that his asssociate possessed many fine qualities. It wasn't long before the two became fast friends.

One of the results of fault-finding and attempting to judge others is that it establishes a negative point of view, which clouds our vision and cankers our souls. On the other hand, looking for the good in others is the positive approach and enhances and manifests the good in our own personalities.

President J. Reuben Clark, Jr., emphasized the importance of leaving judgment to the Lord and of the fact that the Lord judges us with mercy and love. He said:

I have a feeling . . . that when the time comes for passing judgment . . . for every good deed we have done, we shall receive the full reward that it is possible to bestow under the rules and laws governing, and having in mind justice. And I have the further feeling that for every ill thing we do there will be imposed upon us the least penalty that may be bestowed having in mind the principles involved,—eternal justice seasoned with mercy and love.[2]

---

[1]*Pathways to Happiness*, p. 148.

[2]J. Reuben Clark, Jr., *Conference Report*, April 1958, pp. 48-49.

Love
Enduring

. . . Be faithful and diligent in keeping the commandments of God, and I will encircle thee in the arms of my love. (D&C 6:20.)

THE profound love of our Father in heaven for his children here upon the earth runs as a golden thread throughout the scriptures, both ancient and modern. God's love is the magic alchemy that, if we will but let it, can transform the common incidents of life into wonderful experiences for the growth and development of our souls.

We, as earthly parents, are concerned with the welfare and prosperity of our children. We try to rear them in an atmosphere of trust and love, and seek to guide and direct them past the pitfalls and dangers along life's way.

Our Father in heaven, whose love is perfect, is ever mindful of us, his children. Since the beginning of time, he has sought to lead and direct us into paths of righteousness. He has given us the opportunity of coming to this earth so that we might grow and progress through life's experiences. In order that we might dwell with him forever, in his all-encompassing love, "he gave his only begotten

Son, that whosoever believeth in him should not perish, but have everlasting life." (John 3:16.)

We, as parents, particularly appreciate those of our children who, by obedience to the teaching and regulations of our household, show their love for us. "A wise son maketh a glad father. . . ." (Prov. 15:20.) So it is with our Father in heaven. We must hearken unto his word and be obedient to his laws if we expect his love and blessings. He has told us, "I love them that love me. . . ." (Prov. 8:17.) And "If ye love me, keep my commandments." (John 14:15.)

Recently there appeared in a newspaper a picture of a woman with tears streaming down her face, clutching lovingly the flag of the free country in which she had just been granted citizenship. This touching scene has been repeated thousands of times in recent years, when peoples from oppressed lands have found a haven of peace and security in the free countries of the world. In every case, however, before earning the protection of free-land citizenship, it was necessary that these individuals be willing to follow the rules and laws and abide by the "commandments" established by these countries for citizenship. Not one of these individuals gained such privileges and blessings by wishful thinking, or merely by an expression of desire.

In order to gain citizenship in God's kingdom, we must know and follow his laws and commandments. He has repeatedly emphasized this fact by such statements as, "My son, forget not my law; but let thine heart keep my commandments." (Prov. 3:1.) "For the commandment is a lamp; and the law is light. . . ." (Prov. 6:23.)

A warm glow of inner peace and security comes to those who earnestly strive to do the Lord's will and to keep his commandments. For surely these commandments and laws are a lamp and light that shine forth, assuring us an inner freedom from oppression. They hold us to the true course and assure us of the great blessings that the

Lord promised when he said: ". . . Be faithful and diligent in keeping the commandments of God, and I will encircle thee in the arms of my love." (D&C 6:20.)

Certainly there can be no greater blessing than to know that the Lord loves us, and that if we do his will, we will have his arms protectingly about us.

The Magic
Of Love

See that ye love one another; cease to be covetous; learn to impart one to another as the gospel requires. (D&C 88:123.)

T HE charge we have been given to love one another is, without doubt, one of the greatest of the Lord's commandments. He himself described it as the second great commandment, superseded only by the charge to love the Lord.

We all remember the incident described in the scriptures when the lawyer of the Pharisees, tempting Jesus, asked him: "Master, which is the great commandment in the law?" Jesus answered, "Thou shalt love the Lord thy God with all thy heart, and with all thy soul, and with all thy mind. This is the first and great commandment. And the second is like unto it, Thou shalt love thy neighbour as thyself." (Matt. 22:37-39.)

Why is this the greatest of all commandments? Why do all the laws and the prophets hang on this commandment? Why did Jesus say, "A new commandment I give unto you, That ye love one another; as I have loved you"? (John 13:34.)

The obvious answer to these questions is that true love

fulfills all other commandments. A person who really loves the Lord would not think of taking his name in vain nor of having any other gods before him.

If one truly loves another, he would not steal from him and certainly he would not covet what he has. He would be, moreover, sympathetic, understanding, kind, generous, courteous, unselfish, of good temper, and sincere. For, as the apostle Paul wrote: "Charity [meaning the pure love of Christ] suffereth long, and is kind; charity envieth not; charity vaunteth not itself, is not puffed up, Doth not behave itself unseemly, seeketh not her own, is not easily provoked, thinketh no evil." (1 Cor. 13:4-5.) In addition, through true love all of us would "impart one to another as the gospel requires."

Paul classifies love as the greatest of all influences. After describing the gifts of the spirit and the power of faith, and contrasting charity (love) with eloquence, prophecy, and all knowledge, he says that charity is greater than all of these. (1 Cor. 13:1-3.)

How can we learn to keep this commandment to love one another? In answer to this question, someone has remarked, "You learn to speak by speaking, to study by studying, to run by running, and just so, you learn to love by loving."

A modern example of genuine love, as practiced by today's younger generation, was described recently in a letter published in a widely read newspaper column.

The letter, written by a bereaved mother in defense of the behavior of our nation's youth, described the experiences of her family since the tragic death of her seventeen-year-old son.

In her letter she wrote that the response of her friends was overwhelming, but that the real depth of love in action was demonstrated by her son's fellow high school friends. These young people, through personal collections, had a florist make a blanket of flowers in the school colors and established a $400 scholarship in her son's name. Beyond these expressions of love, every day since the funeral, several of these students have stopped in at the home to visit and to learn what they might do to be of assistance.

To paraphrase the apostle James, this is an example of love undefiled, to visit a bereaved mother in her affliction.

If any of us should find it difficult to develop and express our love for someone else, we might begin by thinking about all of the good qualities the person possesses and practice these same virtues in our association with him or her. As the Prophet Joseph Smith once said, "It is a time-honored adage that love begets love. Let us pour forth love—show forth our kindness unto all mankind, and the Lord will reward us with everlasting increase; cast our bread upon the waters and we shall receive it after many days, increased to a hundredfold."[1]

When one truly loves, he gets love in return; moreover he builds, strengthens, purifies, and ennobles his own character and motivates similar attributes in the person loved. This thought was beautifully expressed in a poem entitled "Love."

> *I love you,*
> *Not only for what you are,*
> *But for what I am*
> *When I am with you.*
>
> *I love you,*
> *Not only for what*
> *You have made of yourself,*
> *But for what*
> *You are making of me.*
>
> *I love you*
> *For the part of me*
> *That you bring out . . .*
> *And for drawing out*
> *Into the light*
> *All the beautiful belongings*
> *That no one else had looked*
> *Quite far enough to find.*

I love you because you
Are helping me to make
Of the lumber of my life
Not a tavern
But a temple;
Out of the works
Of my every day
Not a reproach
But a song. . . .
          (Roy Croft)

If we truly wish an abundant life, we must fill it abundantly with love. Love is the secret of health and happiness. It is the essence of faith, hope, and charity.

Love is the greatest thing in the world. Most important, it is readily available to each of us. All we need to do is to reach out and practice it.

Let us strive constantly to "love one another; cease to be covetous; learn to impart one to another as the gospel requires."

---

[1]*Documentary History of the Church*, Vol. 5, p. 517.

The Virtues Of
Meekness And
Steadfastness

*Govern your house in meekness, and be
steadfast.* (D&C 31:9.)

T<small>HIS</small> message from the Doctrine
and Covenants focuses attention on two virtues that can be
employed with remarkable effect in developing our own
characters and in guiding the activities of others. These two
virtues are meekness and steadfastness.

Meekness is a quality frequently mentioned in the
scriptures and described as a most desirable human trait.
In fact, it is one of the few qualities that Jesus attributed
unto himself. He said, ". . . for I am meek and lowly in
heart." (Matt. 11:29.)

Meekness is sometimes confused with docility and lack
of courage. Moses, whom history proves to have been a
man of strong character and outstanding courage, was described as "very meek above all men which were upon
the face of the earth." (Num. 12:3.) Actually, the term meekness means mild of temper, long-suffering, gentle, kind.
Open-mindedness and teachableness are both facets of
meekness. With these attributes it is easy to understand why

the Savior declared, "Blessed are the meek: for they shall inherit the earth." (Matt. 5:5.)

Steadfastness denotes firmness, self-control, consistency, and staunchness. Those who are steadfast exhibit unfaltering determination in the face of adversity. Helen Keller was one of the truly great women of all times. Much of her remarkable stature was achieved through the application of the virtues of meekness and steadfastness both in her own development and through the efforts of her outstanding teacher.

Due to a serious illness, Miss Keller lost her senses of sight and hearing before she was two years of age. Her parents, seeking to lighten the burden of her tragedy, sought the assistance of an able teacher, Ann Sullivan (Macy). This teacher applied the true meaning of meekness and steadfastness in educating and guiding the child. Through the application of these attributes, a miracle was virtually performed. In a very few years, Miss Keller learned to read Braille, to write, and to acquire the difficult ability to speak. By the time she reached her teens, she was as well educated as any normal child of her age. In due time, she graduated with honors from Radcliffe College and then devoted the rest of her life to working with the blind and deaf of the world.

In attaining the high eminence and respect that they enjoyed, Miss Keller and her great teacher, Mrs. Macy, consistently employed meekness, steadfastness, optimism, and faith. Through exercising these virtues, these two noble women inspired, stimulated, and encouraged millions of people in all walks of life throughout the world.

If we would become great powers for good and lead and direct our children and friends in a loving, helpful way, we must govern our homes and lives in meekness. We must strive to be steadfast and consistent in the application of right principles in all our activities. In our association with others, in and outside the home, we should follow the admonition of the Savior, who said, "No power or influence can or ought to be maintained . . . only by persuasion, by long-suffering, by gentleness and meekness, and by love unfeigned." (D&C 121:41.)

The Quality
Of Mercy

I will be merciful unto you. . . .
(D&C 50:16.)

Among all of the Savior's divine attributes, mercy is one of the greatest. Throughout his mortal life he continuously demonstrated this wonderful virtue. In the well-known story of the Good Samaritan, the Savior asked the question as to which of the three passersby was neighbor to the injured man. "And he said, He that shewed mercy on him. Then said Jesus, . . . Go, and do thou likewise." (See Luke 10:30-37.)

The Savior showed compassion and mercy even to those who were not strong enough to follow him. To the rich young man who did not have the courage to sell all his possessions and follow him, Jesus was grieved, but he still showed mercy and did not condemn him. (Mark 10:21.)

In his greatest test, before he died on the cross, the Savior uttered these immortal words of mercy: "Father, forgive them; for they know not what they do." (Luke 23:34.)

The story is told of a well-known sculptor who was

commissioned to do a heroic statue of the Savior. The sculptor was delighted and wanted to make this his best work. He labored almost night and day for months. Finally he finished the clay model of what he considered to be a magnificent figure of the Christ—a commanding statue depicting strength, dominance, and leadership. The clay model was locked in his studio to set and mature.

Sometime later, when the sculptor returned and opened the door to his studio, he was shocked to see that his masterpiece was greatly altered from the way he had left it. Time, weather, and some unknown power had caused the figure to settle; the head had drooped forward, and the arms and hands, which had been high over the head, were now appealingly outstretched. The change had brought an attitude of compassion and mercy into the figure that the sculptor had been unable to accomplish. Reverently the sculptor looked upon this inspired creation and gave it the simple title, "Come unto me."

Mercy is a Christ-like quality that, when it functions in our lives, will bring blessings of happiness both to ourselves and to those to whom we are merciful. In his *Merchant of Venice*, Shakespeare expressed this thought when he said:

> *The quality of mercy is not strained,*
> *It droppeth as the gentle rain from heaven*
> *Upon the place beneath. It is twice blest;*
> *It blesseth him that gives and him that takes.*

The quality of mercy is such an essential part of successful and joyful living that the Lord has given it to us virtually as a commandment. In Luke 6:36 we read, "Be ye therefore merciful, as your Father also is merciful." The Lord also said, "Blessed are the merciful: for they shall obtain mercy." (Matt. 5:7.)

The grand key words of the Relief Society are, "Said Jesus: ye shall do the work which ye see me do." To be merciful unto others is an essential part of this work. In speaking to Relief Society sisters, the Prophet Joseph Smith said, "You should be armed with mercy . . . manifest benevolence." He also said, "If you would have God have mercy on you, have mercy on one another."

As we apply this great principle to our own lives, let us remember that mercy means more than the absence of criticism and judgment. It implies kindness, consideration, understanding; and it seeks the highest possible good for those who might have offended us.

When we practice the qulity of mercy, we exhibit the true application of love to our lives and in our attitude toward others. Then, and only then, are we entitled to the promise of our Redeemer when he said that with everlasting kindness he will have mercy on us. (See 3 Nephi 33:10.)

Obedience,
Heaven's First
Law

*I, the Lord, am bound when ye do what I
say; but when ye do not what I say, ye
have no promise.* (D&C 82:10.)

T<small>HIS</small> statement in the Doctrine
and Covenants is an expression of one of the most fundamental of all divine truths. The promises given to us by
our Father in heaven are immutable. They are based upon
divine law, and, if we are obedient to the conditions he
requires of us, they will be fulfilled completely and ab-
solutely.

The key to receiving the blessings of the Lord's
promise to us is obedience. We are told that "there is a
law, irrevocably decreed in heaven before the foundations
of this world, upon which all blessings are predicated—And
when we obtain any blessing from God, it is by obedience
to that law upon which it is predicated." (D&C 130:20-21.)

Obedience is heaven's first law. It is the foundation of
all success and all accomplishment. It is the doorway that
leads to salvation. Our third Article of Faith tells us that
through the atonement of Christ all mankind may be
saved, but exaltation is conditioned on obedience to the
laws and ordinances of the gospel.

One of the interesting aspects of obedience is that most of us unhesitatingly recognize and seek to obey natural laws. For example, we use the power of electricity to heat and light our homes, run our appliances, and provide us with many varied conveniences. We do this by complying with the laws through which electricity operates. Yet, in respect to the laws that govern spiritual blessings, often, because we do not fully understand them or because the results of obedience to them may not be so direct or immediate, we sometimes question or hesitate. Nevertheless, these spiritual laws are just as real and certain as are the laws of nature.

Every blessing, temporal or spiritual, is firmly based on law and obedience to it. Obedience, like faith, is a source of power. Through obedience we demonstrate our maturity and give concrete evidence of our humility and teachableness.

An impressive example of the power of obedience in relationship to humility and self-discipline is found in the Old Testament, in the story of Naaman, a captain in the Syrian army. Naaman was a great and honorable man who was afflicted with leprosy. He learned of the prophet Elisha, who, through God's power, could heal this dread disease. Accordingly, the captain went to Elisha and sought his blessings.

The prophet told Naaman to go and wash in the Jordan River seven times and his flesh would be made whole. The mighty Syrian was disappointed in these simple instructions. He had expected that Elisha would require him to do something more dramatic. Thereupon, his servants spoke to Naaman, saying, "My father, if the prophet had bid thee do some great thing, wouldest thou not have done it? how much rather then, when he saith to thee, Wash, and be clean?"

Naaman then obeyed Elisha and dipped himself seven times in the river Jordan, and he was healed. (2 Kings 5:14.)

This story illustrates the power of obedience.

Through obedience, not only do we open the doorway to the Lord's blessings but we also demonstrate our love for him. The Savior said, "He that hath my commandments and keepeth them, he it is that loveth me: . . . and I will love him, and will manifest myself to him." (John 14:21.) Jesus also promised us, "If ye keep my commandments, ye shall abide in my love. . . ." (John 15:10.)

Out of his gracious love for us, our Father in heaven has given us laws and commandments that, if obeyed, assure us of his love, guidance, and blessings.

Truly the Lord is bound if we do what he says, but if we do not what he says, we have no promise.

The Refining
Power Of
Patience

*. . . continue in patience until ye are
perfected.* (D&C 67:13.)

I~N HIS~ incomparable Sermon on the
Mount, the Savior gave to us a great yet most difficult
commandment to obey. He said, "Be ye therefore perfect,
even as your Father which is in heaven is perfect." (Matt.
5:48.)

Ever since that time, some 2,000 years ago, conscientious followers of the Lord have been concerned about this
commandment and have wondered if it is possible for imperfect human beings to become as perfect as their Father
in heaven. One answer that has been given to this age-
old question is that as long as one is doing everything possible to become perfect, he is on the road to perfection and,
therefore, doing all that he can to fulfill the Lord's commandment.

Another answer to this question is found in this passage of the 67th section of the Doctrine and Covenants.
The entire verse states, "Ye are not able to abide the presence of God now, neither the ministering of angels; wherefore, continue in patience until ye are perfected."

The importance of exercising patience in reaching perfection is also stated by the great apostle Peter when he, in his second epistle to the saints of his day, admonished them to "add to your faith virtue; and to virtue knowledge; And to knowledge temperance; and to temperance patience; and to patience godliness." (2 Peter 1:5-6.)

Could it be, then, that if we diligently practice the qualities that incorporate the attribute of patience, we may arrive at perfection?

What are these qualities? Some of the more important of these are gentleness, calmness, self-control, long-suffering, and perseverance.

Briefly let us consider each of these as they relate to patience.

Gentleness is a basic characteristic of patience. Patient people are gentle, understanding, thoughtful, and kind. When we practice these traits, we exhibit patience.

Calmness is another characteristic that incorporates patience. A calm person is one who bears the everyday small trials and annoyances quietly and with equanimity. Experience in meeting these small problems this way builds strength to meet and handle the big problems when they come along. All of us can practice this characteristic of patience.

Self-control is one of the most important aspects of patience. One cannot control others until he first controls himself. Self-control means controlling our emotions, our angers, and our appetites. Self-control means self-restraint.

Long-suffering is another attribute of patience. Even the most tranquil life must meet disappointments, discouragements, failures, and defeat. The ability to meet these in fine spirits, high courage, and good humor is an important part of long-suffering. The courage to get up and try again when one has been knocked down and the ability to endure to the end are essential traits of patience.

Perseverance is a handmaiden of patience, without

which perfection is impossible. Perseverance means persistence and steadfastness in achieving worthwhile goals. It is the road to perfection.

Individual patience has played an exceedingly important role in the history and development of the Church. This was particularly true of the pioneer trek westward, when with all of their trials, tribulations, obstacles, and disappointments, the saints bore up patiently and made their triumphant entry into the Salt Lake Valley. During the depth of their discouragement, William R. Clayton composed the great immortal hymn:

> Come, come, ye Saints, no toil nor labor fear;
> But with joy wend your way.
> Though hard to you this journey may appear,
> Grace shall be as your day.
> 'Tis better far for us to strive.
> Our useless cares from us to drive;
> Do this, and joy your hearts will swell—
> All is well! all is well![1]

Someone has wisely said, "Patience strengthens the spirit, sweetens the temper, stifles anger, extinguishes envy, subdues pride, bridles the tongue, restrains the hand."

"Patience is the soul of peace. Of all of the virtues it is the nearest kin to heaven; it makes men look like gods."

---

[1]Latter-day Saints Hymns, No. 13.

Power
Added Upon

For unto him that receiveth it shall be given more abundantly, even power. (D&C 71:6.)

THE entire quotation from which this message in the Doctrine and Covenants is taken states, "Now, behold this is wisdom; whoso readeth, let him understand and receive also; For unto him that receiveth it shall be given more abundantly, even power." (D&C 71: 5-6.)

Those called to proclaim the gospel, expounding the things of the kingdom according to the spirit and power given them, are promised that as they proclaim the gospel truths, more power to teach the gospel will be added unto them.

This promise of being given added ability or power is also referred to by the Savior in these words: "For whosoever hath, to him shall be given, and he shall have more abundance: but whosoever hath not, from him shall be taken away even that he hath." (Matt. 13:12.)

The fulfillment of this promise is realized not only as we preach the gospel, but also as we seek after knowledge, wisdom, and understanding. The assurance of having knowledge added upon knowledge is one of the most gratifying and comforting of life's basic challenges.

One of the interesting characteristics of knowledge is that as we seek and receive it, it comes to us with its own magnifier and multiplier. Truth leads to more truth. Knowledge opens the door to more knowledge, and as one learns, one's capacity to learn improves and one's scope of understanding is broadened. President Heber J. Grant so often emphasized the aphorism of Emerson, "That which we persist in doing becomes easier for us to do; not that the nature of the thing itself is changed, but that our power to do is increased."

President Grant's own life exemplified dramatically the application of this basic truth. He surmounted many unusual difficulties through practice and persistence, by taking one step at a time and by using each mastered step to assist him to take the next one.

The story is well known of how President Grant improved his penmanship from virtual illegibility to beautiful handwriting through persistence and practice. Also, as a small boy he was unable to sing or carry a tune, and those who tried to teach him despaired in their efforts. Yet, through persistent practice and determination, one step at a time, he learned to sing numerous songs and hymns. George D. Pyper, famed musician, once remarked, "President Grant was born with less tune, time, or rhythm than most mortals, yet by his intense energy and persistence, he overcame this handicap."[1]

Certainly as we succeed in performing well one task, our ability to move forward to greater accomplishments is improved. Truly, as the Doctrine and Covenants states, "unto him that receiveth it shall be given more abundantly, even power." (D&C 71:6.)

During his ministry, the Savior lamented the fact that many of the people he attempted to teach, although they had eyes and ears, were unable to see, hear, or understand. Unfortunately, this is also frequently true in our own experience. We refuse to see or to receive knowledge. All too often we allow confusion, complacency, uncertainty, and lack of confidence to blind and cheat us out of the joys and accomplishments that knowledge and understanding can bring.

Some years ago a great woman swimmer who had conquered the English Channel attempted to swim the shorter distance from the California coast to Catalina Island. The water was cold and a heavy fog lay on the ocean. After successfully covering most of the distance, she gave up and asked to be taken into the boat that accompanied her. Sometime later she was asked if, perhaps, a combination of the cold water and the distance had been responsible for her failure. She replied, "No, it was not the cold nor the distance. It was the fog. I became discouraged when I could not see my objective."

Fog—lack of confidence and faith—can easily dim our eyes so that we cannot see our objectives. We become discouraged and close our minds so that we cannot receive wisdom and understanding. As a result, we fail in the accomplishments for which we are actually qualified.

In order to gain the joys that accomplishment and achievement bring, we must keep constantly in mind that one task well done leads to the next and makes its achievement less difficult. We must keep fog, complacency, and uncertainty from dimming our eyes and minds, constantly remembering, as the Lord has promised, that as we progress in wisdom and understanding, it shall be given to us more abundantly.

Like a muscle that grows stronger through exercise, the successful completion of each new task strengthens our ability to meet and accomplish the next. Step by step, as we progress, we receive wisdom and knowledge, and we enhance our ability to gain added strength and power.

---

[1]Bryant S. Hinckley, *Life of a Great Leader*, p. 48.

Ask and Receive

Ask, and ye shall receive; knock, and it shall
be opened unto you. (D&C 66:9.)

For our own happiness, for our
own growth and development, there is probably no counsel
given to us by the Lord that is more important than that
given in this quotation from the Doctrine and Covenants.
In order to receive the Lord's blessings, we must seek
them, for he has told us, "Ask, and ye shall receive; knock,
and it shall be opened unto you." (D&C 66:9.) In fact, so
important is this counsel that the Lord has emphasized
it repeatedly in all the dispensations of his gospel.

Anciently, through his prophets, he pleaded with his
people not to forsake him but to seek him constantly.
Moses challenged his people not to leave the Lord, saying,
". . . is not he thy father . . . hath he not made thee, and
established thee? . . . ask thy father, and he will shew
thee. . . ." (Deut. 32:6-7.) Solomon expressed the same
thought when he said, "In all thy ways acknowledge him,
and he shall direct thy paths." (Prov. 3:6.) Through the
prophet Jeremiah the Lord said, "Call unto me, and I will
answer thee. . . ." (Jer. 33:3.)

In his Sermon on the Mount, the Lord Jesus Christ once more extended to his people the same glorious invitation: "Ask, and it shall be given you; seek, and ye shall find; knock, and it shall be opened unto you."

And then the Lord added, "For every one that asketh receiveth; and he that seeketh findeth; and to him that knocketh it shall be opened.

"Or what man is there of you, whom if his son ask bread, will he give him a stone? . . .

"If ye then, being evil, know how to give good gifts unto your children, how much more shall your Father which is in heaven give good things to them that ask him?" (Matt. 7:7-11.)

When the Savior organized his church among the Nephites on the American continent, he emphasized this same counsel and invitation. (See 3 Nephi 14:7-8.) Then, to dramatize the importance of this counsel further, just prior to his ascension to heaven, the Savior again said, ". . . whatsoever things ye shall ask the Father in my name shall be given unto you.

"Therefore, ask, and ye shall receive; knock, and it shall be opened unto you. . . ." (3 Nephi 27:28-29.)

Why is this counsel or invitation so important that the Lord has emphasized and reemphasized it so repeatedly?

One of the best answers to this question was given by Isaiah when he described some of the blessings the Lord has in store for those who ask and wait upon the Lord. He said, ". . . men have not heard . . . neither hath the eye seen . . . what he [the Lord] hath prepared for him that waiteth for him." (Isa. 64:4.)

The apostle Paul restated this same promise in a letter to the Corinthians. He said. "Eye hath not seen, nor ear heard, neither have entered into the heart of man, the things which God hath prepared for them that love him." (1 Cor. 2:9.)

Wonderful blessings, blessings beyond our power to

comprehend, are prepared by the Lord for us if we will conscientiously seek them. But to seek them, we must ask; to enter into the Lord's house of promise, we must knock. The apostle James told the early Christians, ". . . ye have not, because ye ask not." (James 4:1.) However, these blessings do not come automatically. We must be deserving and we must ask in faith, "nothing wavering." (See James 1:6.) The Savior said, ". . . all things, whatsoever ye shall ask in prayer, believing, ye shall receive." (Matt. 21:22.)

One famous author has set down four requirements necessary when asking for blessings from the Lord. He said, "Test your desire. Is it good for you? Are you ready for it now? Is it fair to all others concerned? Do you honestly feel it is according to God's will?"[1] If we can truly answer "yes" to these four questions, we can ask the Lord for our desires. But we must ask him with full, unwavering faith, believing.

There is still another requirement if we are to receive the Lord's blessings. This requirement was emphasized in an experience shared by the Prophet Joseph Smith and Oliver Cowdery while they were working on the translation of the Book of Mormon. At one point in that work, Oliver, with the permission of the Prophet, attempted to translate but was unable to use the urim and thummim, and he and Joseph inquired of the Lord the reason. In answer, the Lord said, "Behold, you have not understood; you have supposed that I would give it unto you, when you took no thought save it was to ask me. But, behold, I say unto you, that you must study it out in your mind; then you must ask me if it be right, and if it is right I will cause that your bosom shall burn within you; therefore, you shall feel that it is right." (D&C 9:7-8.)

As indicated in this experience, the Lord also expects us to work and to exercise our own intelligence and initiative in order to deserve his blessings.

Surely the Lord has prepared for us bounteous

blessings. He pleads with us to live so as to deserve these blessings; and, deserving them, he counsels us to "ask, and ye shall receive; knock, and it shall be opened unto you." But let us be wise in that which we request. Let us be sure that we have done what the Lord requires, asking in faith — fully believing. Then the Lord will open the doors of his rich blessings and shower them up-on us.

---

[1]Charles L. Allen, *How to Get What You Want*, p. 79.

Prayer, An Open Channel To Heaven

Pray always, and I will pour out my Spirit upon you, and great shall be your blessing. . . . (D&C 19:38.)

OUR Father in heaven, in his deep, eternal love for his children, has given us a special, priceless blessing. This blessing is the right and privilege to communicate with him in prayer. Through prayer we have a constant opportunity to call on him for guidance, inspiration, and wisdom. Through this divine communication we can strengthen our courage to meet, understand, and solve life's many problems. The Lord has invited us to partake of the spiritual strength that comes from constant, sincere communication with him. He has promised us: "And all things, whatsoever ye shall ask in prayer, believing, ye shall receive." (Matt. 21:22.)

Many of us, however, go through life without taking full advantage of this wonderful invitation. Even those of us who pray regularly too often allow our prayers to develop into stereotyped rituals. We allow them to become repetitive and impersonal. We fall into the habit of going through the physical motions of prayer without really communicating with God. Such prayers, unfortunately, consist chiefly of meaningless words that lack the real spirit of divine communication. In *Hamlet,* Shakespeare decries this tendency:

> *My words fly up, my thoughts remain below . . .*
> *Words without thoughts never to heaven go.*

Another weakness some of us exhibit in our prayers consists in the habit of coming to the Lord only under urgent circumstances when we are in frantic need of his help. We tend to forget him when things move along pleasantly and successfully.

In order for the Lord to pour out his Spirit upon us, our prayers must be offered in faith and sincerity and must come from our hearts. We must approach our Heavenly Father with a contrite and humble spirit, feeling and expressing our complete dependency upon him. Someone has said that when we feel the least like praying is when we should pray the most.

President Heber J. Grant expressed the need for constant sincere prayer when he said:

> *The minute a man stops supplicating God for his spirit and direction, just so soon he starts out to become a stranger to him and his work. When men stop praying for God's spirit, they place confidence in their own unaided reason, and they gradually lose the spirit of God just the same as dear friends, by never writing to, or visiting with each other, will become strangers.*[1]

The importance of constant prayer was vividly emphasized by the great Book of Mormon prophet Amulek, who said: "Yea, humble yourselves, and continue in prayer unto him." (Alma 34:19.) "Yea, and when you do not cry unto the Lord, let your hearts be full, drawn out in prayer unto him continually for your welfare, and also for the welfare of these who are around you." (Alma 34:27.)

In a conference with missionaries in Great Britain,

one of our present-day apostles remarked that he had observed that many of the missionaries had not learned the simple secret of carrying a prayer always in their hearts not only for their own welfare but for the welfare of those around them. Consequently, these missionaries were experiencing only a taste of the great blessings and rich guidance in store for them.

The story is told of a man who had traveled extensively and had seen the beauties and wonders of the world. He had met and made friends with influential and interesting people throughout the world and felt that his life was full. Then he embraced the gospel. For the first time in his life he learned to pray. Gradually he learned the meaning of true prayer and the happiness that comes to those who, at all times, carry a prayer in their hearts. He said:

> *In retrospect my life was dark and empty compared to the real beauty and meaning of life today. Now I have learned the joy which comes to those who keep in close communication with the Lord. My life before was like the flicker movies of the 1920's compared with the colorful cinemascope of today.*

Constant prayer results in rich and radiant living. It generates spiritual strength and courage that can be attained from no other source. What greater blessing exists in this world than the choice opportunity of enjoying constant companionship with the Lord's spirit? This wonderful privilege is ours if we follow the simple admonition:

> *Pray always, and I will pour out my Spirit upon you, and great shall be your blessing. . . .*

---

[1]*The Improvement Era*, August 1944, p. 481.

Seek The
Lord Early

*He that seeketh me early shall find me,
and shall not be forsaken.* (D&C 88:83.)

Both King David and his son Solomon realized the wisdom of seeking and finding the Lord early in their lives. David, the psalmist, sang, "O God, thou art my God; early will I seek thee. . . ." (Ps. 63:1.) Solomon records, "I [the Lord] love them that love me; and those that seek me early shall find me." (Prov. 8:17.)

David, who became one of the greatest of all Israel's kings, sought the Lord while he was very young and thus became a chosen vessel. When the great prophet Samuel, who had also sought and found the Lord early, was searching for a future king to take Saul's place, he came to Bethlehem. By commandment of the Lord he sought one of Jesse's seven sons. Jesse, the proud father, brought his sons before Samuel and thought surely the Lord would choose his eldest. "But the Lord said unto Samuel, Look not on his countenance, or on the height of his stature; . . . for the Lord seeth not as man seeth; for man looketh on the outward appearance, but the Lord looketh on the heart." (1 Sam. 16:7.)

The Lord had chosen David because he had sought him early while still a boy, and his heart was fully in tune with the Lord's Spirit.

When Solomon, as a very young man, was selected to succeed his father, David, as the king of Israel, he too had sought and found the Lord early in his life: "And Solomon loved the Lord, walking in the statutes of David his father. . . ." (1 Kings 3:3.)

In response to the Lord's call, Solomon said, "And now, O Lord my God, thou has made thy servant king instead of David my father: and I am but a little child; I know not how to go out or come in." (1 Kings 2:7.) Solomon then petitioned the Lord that he be given an understanding heart so that he would be wise in judging and guiding his people.

It is a significant fact that many of the great leaders in the Lord's work have sought and found the Savior early in their lives. Jesus himself was about his Father's business when he was only twelve. The Prophet Joseph Smith opened the door for the restoration of the gospel and ushered in the dispensation of the fulness of times when he was only fourteen.

Why is it that the Lord admonishes us to seek him early? Surely one reason is that in our youth our minds and spirits are more malleable and teachable. At an early age our minds are not cluttered with misinformation, which builds doubt and skepticism. Obviously another reason is that the earlier we seek and find the Lord, the longer we will have to grow and develop under the influence of his Spirit.

Parents have the obligation to encourage their children to seek the Lord early in their lives. Habits established in youth tend to persist and form the permanent character of the individual.

Not only should we seek the Lord early in life, but we should also seek him early each day. All of us need the

Lord's Spirit all day, every day. President Hugh B. Brown, at a Relief Society conference, quoted the following:

> *I meet God in the morning*
> *When my day is at its best,*
> *And his presence comes like sunshine,*
> *Like a glory in my breast.*
> *All day long his presence lingers,*
> *All day long he stays with me;*
> *And we sail in perfect calmness*
> *O'er a sometimes troubled sea.*
> *So I think I know a secret,*
> *Learned from traveling down life's way—*
> *You must seek God in the morning*
> *If you want him through the day.*[1]

Certainly the presence of the Lord's Spirit is a great blessing, and we should seek to enjoy it as early as possible. We must not procrastinate. As the prophet Amulek declared, ". . . I beseech of you that ye do not procrastinate the day of your repentance. . . ." (Alma 34:33.) And through his modern Prophet, the Lord has declared, " . . . behold, I come quickly, . . . and they who have sought me early shall find rest to their souls." (D&C 54:10.)

The important conclusion we must draw from this instruction from our Father in heaven is that we must seek the Lord earnestly and diligently every day if we expect to find him. Under his divine plan of personal free agency, he will not force himself upon us. He will come to us only if we sincerely and wholeheartedly *seek* him.

---

[1] *Relief Society Magazine*, December 1965, p. 886.

Teach Us To Pray

. . . he that prayeth, whose spirit is contrite, the same is accepted of me. . . .
(D&C 52:15.)

Prayer is truly "the soul's sincere desire." Probably no other human motivating force is as universally present in the spirit of man as is the desire to draw near to our Father in heaven and to seek his divine comfort and help. Although some self-sufficient individuals may not feel the need for prayer until faced with a great personal crisis or seemingly insoluble problem, the need to seek the Lord's help is still probably one of the most compelling forces that exists in the human spirit.

Even those of us who make a habit of prayer often feel that we lack the knowledge of how to draw near to our Heavenly Father so that we are sure he will hear and answer the pleadings of our hearts. Like the disciples of old, many of us cry out, "Lord, teach us to pray." (Luke 11:1.)

The Lord has answered this plea many times and in many ways. In our modern scripture he tells us specifically what to do if our prayers are to be acceptable unto him. He admonishes us to come to him with a contrite spirit.

But, we say, what does he mean by a contrite spirit? The answer is given in many places throughout the scriptures. For example, through his prophet Jeremiah, the Lord spoke these words: "And ye shall seek me, and find me, when ye shall search for me with all your heart." (Jer. 29:13.) To Solomon the Lord said, "If my people . . . shall humble themselves, and pray, and seek my face, and turn from their wicked ways; then will I hear from heaven. . . ." (2 Chron. 7:14.)

The Book of Mormon prophet Alma tells us to " . . . acknowledge your unworthiness before God at all times" (Alma 38:14), and, in the Doctrine and Covenants, the Lord instructs us, "Draw near unto me and I will draw near unto you; seek me diligently and ye shall find me" (D&C 88:63).

From these scriptures we learn that in order to pray with a contrite spirit, we must search for the Lord with all our hearts and with complete humility. We must draw near to the Lord if we expect him to draw near to us, and we must seek him with sincerity and diligence. Furthermore, we must acknowledge our weaknesses and faults before him in full repentance.

It is not easy to learn to pray with a contrite spirit. Yet the blessings that come from such prayers are worth the most conscientious and dedicated efforts.

To pray with contriteness, we must cleanse our hearts and souls of such human weaknesses as envy, jealousy, malice, and strife. We cannot draw near to our Father in heaven if we are angry with our neighbor or if we have a feeling of hatred in our hearts. We must search our souls for our imperfections and shortcomings, acknowledge them freely before the Lord, and ask for his mercy and forgiveness. This does not mean that we should dwell unnecessarily on our weaknesses. Rather, we should make our prayers constructive and cast our burdens at the feet of the Lord, knowing that an all-wise Father knows our shortcomings and the sincerity of our desire to correct them. Someone has said that "when the soul has laid down its faults at the feet of God, it feels as though it had wings."

One of the classic examples in scripture of how to pray with a contrite spirit is told by the Savior in the parable of the pharisee and the publican. The pharisee prayed, ". . . I thank thee, that I am not as other men are, extortioners, unjust, adulterers. . . . I fast twice in the week, I give tithes of all I possess." The publican, standing afar off, offered his prayer in only seven simple words, in abject humility. He pleaded, "God be merciful to me a sinner." The Savior said that this was the type of prayer that was acceptable to him. (See Luke 18:10-13.)

When we pray, let us avoid the temptation of attempting to bargain with the Lord. We should not be guilty of telling the Lord that if he will give us certain blessings, we will fulfill certain promises. By such an approach we lay bare our insincerity. The Lord knows what is in our hearts, and he does not seek our promises in exchange for his blessings. There is no sham or pretense in a contrite spirit. When we approach the Lord with all our hearts, our whole personality and character is laid bare in our earnest desire to draw near to him and enjoy his blessings.

It is the sincerity, earnestness, and contriteness of our hearts that counts when we pray and not the multiplying of words or the repeating of trite phrases. Let us remember that the Lord has said, "I know thy heart, and have heard thy prayers. . . ." (D&C 112:11.)

The Comfort
Of Prayer

Pray always, that ye may not faint."
(D&C 88:126.)

No MATTER how self-confident or self-sufficient one may think he is, every person has need for additional help and direction beyond that which human power can provide. This need can be fulfilled through the strength and help that come from communion with our Father in heaven through earnest, sincere prayer.

Sincere prayer provides a sustaining strength and support that can come from no other source. It enriches and steadies life. It adds hope, tranquility, peace, patience, and courage. It gives assurance of the presence of a powerful and comforting Friend who is near and desirous of giving help. President McKay has said, "Prayer is the pulsation of a yearning, loving heart in tune with the Infinite. It is a message of the soul sent directly to a loving Father. The language is not mere words but spirit-vibration."[1]

The scriptures repeatedly testify that we must "ask . . . seek . . . knock." (Matt. 7:7.) We must initiate the request if we expect to receive the Lord's blessings and to have the assurance of his guidance and help. It is true that the Lord ". . . knows the desires of our hearts before we ask, but he has made it obligatory, and a duty that we shall call upon his name."[2]

Why does the Lord tell us to "pray always, that ye may not faint"? According to the dictionary, one who faints is one who is wanting in courage; lacking in strength; weak, feeble, and dejected.

Our Father in heaven knows our weaknesses, our need for courage and strength. In fact, in the scriptures he reminds us that without the presence of his Spirit and his support, we can do nothing. (See John 15:5.) Even the Savior confirmed his constant dependence upon his Father. He repeatedly declared that his mighty works were performed by the power of God's Spirit and he made it clear that "I can of mine own self do nothing: . . . I seek not mine own will, but the will of the Father which hath sent me." (John 5:30.)

One of the glorious blessings of prayer is that through it none of us need lack courage or hope, or be weak or faint. Prayer enables us to tap a vast, unseen reservoir of strength and to bring to the daily problems and cares of life sustaining support and wise solutions.

Even more than this, prayer is a force as real as the powers of gravity. In fact, at times it seems to have the power to control or even to supersede the laws of nature. Many of us have experienced this power in the miracles of healing or in the remarkably comforting effects of consolation that have occurred in crises in our families. At times, through prayer, we have been given strength well beyond the scope of our human capacities.

For example, recently on a dark, cold night on an icy bend in the road, a car skidded and overturned into an embankment below. The lone driver, seriously hurt, instinctively knew she would die if help did not come immediately. She received no response to her frantic cries or the sounding of her car's horn. All this time she was praying mightily; and finally, with the sustaining strength that flowed into her body, she crawled to the road above.

Later, in the hospital, the doctor wanted to know who had been in the car with her; he was unbelieving when she insisted she had been alone. But she said, "Actually, I was not alone, for God was with me, and he helped me back up to the road."

The doctor replied, "He must have been with you. You could not have climbed onto the road alone. You have a broken back."

Through prayer, miracles are performed. If we are humble, believing, and prayerful, no matter what the circumstances, we are never actually alone. If we are deserving, we have the Lord's promise that his Spirit will always be with us. This is why we should "pray always, that ye may not faint."

The poet Alfred Lord Tennyson expressed this thought beautifully when he wrote:

> More things are wrought by prayer
> Than the world dreams of.
> Wherefore, let thy voice rise like a fountain for me night and day.
> For what are men better than sheep and goats, . . .
> If, knowing God, they lift not hands of prayer
> Both of themselves and those who call them friends,
> For so the whole round earth is every way
> Bound by gold chains about the feet of God.
>
> (Morte D' Arthur.)

---

[1] Pathways to Happiness, p. 225.
[2] Joseph F. Smith, Gospel Doctrine, p. 221.

Beware of Pride

. . . beware of pride, lest thou shouldst enter
into temptation. (D&C 23:1.)

REPEATEDLY in his teachings, our Father in heaven warns us of the danger of selfish pride. In his all-seeing wisdom he knows that our spiritual development and our joy and success depend upon humility, meekness, modesty, understanding, and a constant striving for self-development and improvement.

Selfish pride generates opposite characteristics. It provides vanity, arrogance, haughtiness, covetousness, boastfulness, and other negative characteristics. These limit and stifle growth and stand as obstacles to successful living.

The Book of Mormon prophet Alma expressed his concern about pride when he advised his son Shiblon to "see that ye are not lifted up unto pride; yea, see that ye do not boast in your own wisdom, nor of your much strength." (Alma 38:11.)

This great prophet further warned that those who are lifted up in the pride of their own eyes are led into all manner of wickedness. (See Alma 1:32.)

Solomon, in describing the seven things that "the Lord hates," lists first "a proud look" and emphasizes that "only by pride cometh contention" (Prov. 13:10), and "before destruction the heart of man is haughty . . ." (Prov. 18:12).

The Lord's deep concern that we should beware of pride lest we enter into temptation is a warning against selfish pride. Selfish pride leads to self-aggrandizement and becomes Satan's tool of temptation. Even Jesus was not spared Satan's clever temptation aimed at an appeal to selfish pride. Prior to the Savior's ministry, the devil took

> . . . him up into an exceeding high mountain, and sheweth him all the kingdoms of the world, and the glory of them;
>
> And saith unto him, All these things will I give thee, if thou wilt fall down and worship me.
>
> Then saith Jesus unto him, Get thee hence, Satan. . . . (Matt. 4:8-10.)

Pride can lead to the destruction not only of individuals but of whole nations. This destructive power is particularly evident in Book of Mormon history. When the people kept the commandments of the Lord, they prospered. But during periods of prosperity, they often allowed themselves to become "proud in their hearts. . . ." (4 Nephi 43.) It was under these conditions that they succumbed to Satan's temptations and were led to their own destruction.

Unselfish pride, if properly controlled and channeled, may exert a constructive influence. For example, we should never undermine our own self-respect and dignity. We should be proud of our divine heritage as children of our Father in heaven and as descendants of worthy parents. We have the right to be proud of the righteous accomplishments of our children and of the blessings and opportunities of membership in our great Church. These evidences of unselfish pride are good as long as they serve as incentives to more purposeful living.

Yet this unselfish pride too can also become a tool of temptation in Satan's hand. Unless it is controlled, it can lead to a sense of self-sufficiency, to self-righteousness and intolerance. These attitudes can constrict and limit our development. They can make us unteachable and wise in our own eyes. They can make us resistant to the teachings and counsels of the Lord and can cause us to slip backward rather than to move forward.

We need not be rich or powerful or achieve worldly fame and honor in order to encounter the destroying influences of pride. None of us is immune to this human weakness. Pride raises its tempting head throughout each day's activities. Sometimes it takes the form of stubbornness. For example, we may hesitate to ask forgiveness of another when we speak a harsh word or fail to do some little kind act, because our pride stands in the way. We may become jealous of another's accomplishment or of some honor he or she may have received, because our pride impresses us that we might have done as well. Sometimes our pride makes us unwilling to accept the wise advice of others and hinders us from applying better ways of doing things.

Surely all of us need constantly to keep on guard lest the weakening influence of pride unsuspectingly leads us into temptation. Let us remember the words of Solomon, who said: "Pride goeth before destruction, and an haughty spirit before a fall." (Prov. 16:17.)

How may we then combat the insidious influence of pride?

The Lord has reminded:

He hath shewed thee, O man, what is good; and what doth the Lord require of thee, but to do justly, and to love mercy, and to walk humbly with thy God? (Micah 6:8.)

The Miracle
Of Repentance

Behold, he who has repented of his sins, the
same is forgiven, and I, the Lord, remember
them no more. (D&C 58:42.)

ONE of the most gracious and
generous promises that comes to us from our Father in
heaven is the divine blessing of repentance coupled with
forgiveness. It is a wonderfully encouraging and stimu-
lating conviction to know that if we sincerely and genuinely repent of our faults, errors, and sins, they will be forgiven by the great and final Judge, our Father in heaven,
and "shall be as white as snow" (Isa. 1:18).

Truly this is a marvelous blessing that comes to us
from the goodness of God. As the apostle Paul said, ". . . the
goodness of God leadeth thee to repentance." (Romans 2:4.)
If it were not for this "goodness," all of us would remain
forever in our sins, and we would be unable to move forward toward more useful, purposeful, and effective lives.

What is the meaning of true repentance? How does
it lay the foundation for progress and for more satisfying
and useful lives? The process of repentance has been said
to consist of the application of the four "R's": *recognition,*
remorse, resolve, and restitution.

The first step in true repentance consists in a genuine recognition of our faults. After we recognize our mistakes, the next step follows naturally—we must be sorry and regret them. Then comes a genuine desire and resolve to eliminate them and, finally, to make full and complete restitution. President Joseph F. Smith expressed this thought beautifully when he said:

> . . . *true repentance is not only sorrow for sins, and humble penitence and contrition before God, but it involves the necessity of turning away from them, a discontinuance of all evil practices and deeds, a thorough reformation of life, a vital change from evil to good, from vice to virtue, from darkness to light. Not only so, but to make restitution, so far as is possible, for all the wrongs we have done, to pay our debts, and restore to God and man their rights—that which is due to them from us. This is true repentance, and the exercise of the will and all the powers of body and mind is demanded, to complete this glorious work of repentance; then God will accept it.*[1]

According to an ancient account, a man in a far eastern country was caught stealing. As a part of his punishment, a large "S" was branded on his forehead. Applying the great gift of repentance, he overcame his sin and lived a life of virtue and service in his community. Some years later a stranger asked one of his friends the meaning of the "S" that had been burned into his forehead. The friend replied, "I don't really know, but judging by his life, I'm sure it must stand for 'Saint.' "

Every day we live there is room for repentance. Every one of us needs constantly to be cleansed by this purifying principle, for we read, ". . . there is not a just man upon earth, that doeth good, and sinneth not." (Eccl. 7:20.) The apostle John reemphasized this truth when he said, "If we say that we have no sin, we deceive ourselves, and the truth is not in us." (1 John 1:8.)

Probably one of the greatest difficulties we encounter

in repenting lies in the rationalization of our so-called "little sins." Most of us have consciences that are sufficiently sharp to bring us remorse when we make big mistakes. Our so-called "little" sins, however, such as jealousy, malice, gossip, fault finding, and similar weaknesses, are easy to rationalize, cover up, and forget.

If we truly are going to repent, we should follow the admonition of the ancient apostles, who said to lay aside "all malice, and all guile, and hypocrisies, and envies, and all evil speakings" (1 Peter 2:1), and "Put on therefore . . . kindness, humbleness of mind, meakness, longsuffering; Forbearing one another, and forgiving one another." (Col. 3: 12-13.)

Repentance has a purifying power because associated with it and as a fundamental part of it is the glorious principle of forgiveness. As the Lord has promised in the Doctrine and Covenants, "he who has repented of his sins, the same is forgiven, and I, the Lord, remember them no more." (D&C 58:42.) Milton has said that forgiveness and repentance are "the golden keys that open the palace of eternity."

---

[1]*Journal of Discourses*, Vol. 19, p. 190.

The Rewards
Of Righteousness

*. . . he who doeth the works of righteousness
shall receive his reward.* (D&C 59:23.)

In this quotation from the Doctrine
and Covenants, marvelous blessings are promised to those
who are righteous. The Lord says that "he who doeth the
works of righteousness shall receive his reward, even peace
in this world, and eternal life in the world to come."
(D&C 59:23.)

One of the most impressive examples of the rewards
of righteousness is contained in the story of Job. Job was
a rich man, but despite his worldly abundance, he lived
righteously. In fact, he was described as "perfect and
upright, and one that feared God, and eschewed evil."

On one occasion, some of the Lord's angels came before him, and Satan stood among them. When the Lord
saw Satan, he asked him what he was doing and where he
had been. Satan replied that he had just come from walking over the earth, looking for a good man. The Lord asked
him if he had seen Job, who was perfect and who loved the
Lord. Satan's response was that Job was good because the

Lord had blessed him so bounteously. If these blessings were taken away from him, Satan challenged, Job would rise up and curse the Lord to his face.

So certain was the Lord of Job's faithfulness that he gave Satan the power to take all of Job's blessings away from him, knowing that Job would remain steadfast. Consequently, one by one of Job's possessions—his worldly wealth, his sons, family and servants, even his health—were taken away from him. Yet this faithful man did not falter. He declared, "My righteousness I hold fast, and will not let it go: my heart shall not reproach me so long as I live. . . . I put on righteousness, and it clothed me."

After Job had faithfully withstood all of Satan's tests, the Lord took the evil one's power away from him and blessed Job with twice as much as he had before. Job lived with the Lord's blessings for a hundred and forty years and enjoyed his children and his children's children, "even for four generations."

The word *righteousness,* used extensively throughout the scriptures, is a word all of us feel that we understand. Yet, when we speak of a person as being righteous, are we thinking in specific or in general terms? Do we know the specific qualities or "works" of which righteousness is composed? If we seek to do the works of righteousness, how can we develop the qualities that will lead to such works?

A good description of a righteous person is to be found in the Old Testament in David's first psalm, which states, "Blessed is the man that walketh not in the counsel of the ungodly, nor standeth in the way of sinners, nor sitteth in the seat of the scornful.

"But his delight is in the law of the Lord; and in his law doth he meditate day and night." (Ps. 1:1-2.)

In the New Testament, the Lord's Sermon on the Mount outlines most clearly the specific qualities of righteousness. Some of the more important of these are love, meekness, mercy, pureness of heart and mind, peace-making, forgiveness, tolerance, chastity, faithfulness, constancy, prayerfulness, kindness, charity, humility, and benevolence. This is a rather inclusive list and one that offhand might appear overpowering. Nevertheless, we can find comfort and assurance in the fact that we will be moving toward the desired goal of righteous living if we are doing conscientiously all we can to practice these virtues in our lives.

One of the choice effects of righteous living is found in Fourth Nephi in the Book of Mormon. Following the Savior's visit with the Nephite peoples and the establishment of his church among them, the people lived in righteousness for approximately 200 years. During this period, ". . . they did walk after the commandments which they had received from their Lord. . . .

". . . there was no contention in the land, because of the love of God which did dwell in the hearts of the people.

"And there were no envyings, nor strifes, nor tumults . . . and surely there could not be a happier people among all the people who had been created by the hand of God. . . .

"And how blessed were they! For the Lord did bless them in all their doings. . . ." (4 Nephi 12:15-16, 18.)

No nation and no community is any stronger than the righteousness of the individuals of which it is composed. This was true during the two-hundred-year period after the Savior's visit to the American continent, and it is true today. Another Nephite prophet said, ". . . if there be no righteousness there be no happiness." (2 Nephi 2:13.)

How can we individually do the works of righteousness and thus lay the foundation for happiness and peace in our own lives? We can practice a little more kindness. We can show more love and consideration to our families, friends, and neighbors. We can be tolerant and charitable, and, through prayer, we can seek more diligently the divine will of our Father in heaven. The practice of these and other qualities of righteousness will bring us more peace of mind and more joy of living.

President George Albert Smith stated this basic truth beautifully when he said: "Surely there is nothing men need more than the blessing of peace and happiness and hearts free from fear. . . . The Lord [has] repeated what he has said so many times, the price of peace and happiness is righteousness."[1]

---

[1]Brigham Young University address, December 1949.

Satan's Buffetings

Watch, for the adversary spreadeth his do-
minions. . . . (D&C 82:5.)

SINCE the war in heaven, when Satan and his hosts were cast out, their evil influence has struggled continuously to capture men's souls and to thwart the Lord's work. Evil has always been in the world, but the adversary has been particularly aggressive in attempting to spread his dominion during those periods when the priesthood has been on the earth.

This is undoubtedly why, since the restoration of the gospel, we have been repeatedly warned to watch and be alert to the temptations of the evil one. Never during the history of the world has the kingdom of our Father in heaven progressed more rapidly. Consequently, probably more than at any other time in history, the adversary has marshaled his forces to obstruct it.

Our modern lives are crowded with temptations. Pressures are brought to bear upon us from all directions— the advertisements we read, the radio, television, movies, books, and plays—all of these, at times, in a variety of ways, tempt us to lower the quality of our morals and to give in a little here and a little there on our standards and principles.

These are the devious ways the adversary employs to ensnare us little by little until he has us completely in his power. These are the little temptations that are made enticing and attractive and seem so harmless in and of themselves. These are probably the things about which the prophet Nephi warned us when he said that in latter days, there would be many who would say:

> Eat, drink, and be merry; nevertheless, fear God—he will justify in committing a little sin; yea, lie a little, take the advantage of one because of his words, dig a pit for thy neighbor; there is no harm in this; and do all these things, for tomorrow we die; and if it so be that we are guilty, God will beat us with a few stripes, and at last we shall be saved in the kingdom of God. (2 Nephi 28:8.)

The devil has always worked thus. He knows that if he can encourage us to take a few "little steps" in his direction, he may ensnare us and lead us the whole way. This is why we must be eternally vigilant against the temptations of such things as haughtiness, envy, and pride, of giving vent to uncontrolled irritations or angers, of succumbing to the demoralizing effects of selfishness and jealousy. We should avoid the inhibiting effects of discouragement and doubt and should cleanse our minds and attitudes from fault-finding and contention. These are some of the so-called "little," easy-to-slip-into character weaknesses that dull the conscience and make it easier to yield to the bigger things that eventually will lead us away from the Spirit of our Father in heaven.

In our vigilance against enticements of the adversary, let's be aware of our own individual weaknesses, recognizing that the evil one seeks to tempt us where we are most vulnerable.

Let us follow the counsel of the Savior and not be led into temptation. Let us keep as far away from evil as possible.

The story is told of an employer, during the days of the Old West, who summoned several drivers into his office to interview each with the idea of hiring one of them to drive his stagecoach.

"How close can you drive to the edge of the cliff without going over?" he asked one potential driver.

"Sir, I can come within a foot of the cliff without going over," the man answered unhesitatingly.

"And you, how close can you drive to the edge of the cliff without going over?"

"Why, I can come within six inches of the cliff without going over."

Having heard the questions and answers of the first two, the third man, when asked, replied reluctantly, "Sir, I'd keep as far away from the edge of that cliff as possible!"

This answer convinced the employer that he had found the right man for the job.

And so it is with evil. We should keep as far as possible from it.[1]

Despite the buffetings of Satan and the temptations he throws in our paths we should remember that these are a part of the Lord's plan for our growth and development. "Temptation, is an important factor in man's probation; for by resisting it, the soul is developed and made stronger."[2]

In teaching his sons, the prophet Lehi explained this eternal principle when he said:

> For it must needs be, that there is an opposition in all things. If not so . . . righteousness could not be brought to pass. . . .
> . . . If ye shall say there is no sin, ye shall also say there is no righteousness. And if there be no righteousness there be no happiness. . . .

. . . Wherefore, man could not act for himself save it should be that he was enticed by the one or the other. (2 Nephi 2:11, 13, 16.)

How can we fortify ourselves so that we can clearly distinguish good from evil and avoid being enticed by evil influences? The Book of Mormon prophet Mormon told us how we might know good from evil:

. . . the Spirit of Christ is given to every man, that he may know good from evil; wherefore, I show unto you the way to judge; for every thing which inviteth to do good, and to persuade to believe in Christ, is sent forth by the power and gift of Christ; wherefore ye may know with a perfect knowledge it is of God.

But whatsoever thing persuadeth men to do evil, and believe not in Christ . . . and serve not God, then ye may know with a perfect knowledge it is of the devil. . . . (Moroni 7:16-17.)

President Brigham Young told us how we could overcome evil; he said, "When temptations come to you, be humble and faithful, and determined that you will overcome, and you will receive a deliverance."[3] The great prophet Alma also instructed men to "humble yourselves before the Lord, and call on his holy name, and watch and pray continually, that ye may not be tempted above that which ye can bear. . . ." (Alma 13:28.)

Let us heed the warnings of the Lord and his servants and continually be on guard, watching, "for the adversary spreadeth his dominion."

---

[1]Albert L. Zobell, Jr., Comp., *Story Teller's Scrapbook*, p. 51.
[2]Orson F. Whitney, *Saturday Night Thoughts*, p. 310.
[3]*Discourses of Brigham Young*, p. 82.

Search
The Scriptures

And the Book of Mormon and the holy scriptures are given of me for your instruction. . . . (D&C 33:16.)

In the Doctrine and Covenants, 33:16, the Lord declared that he has preserved our holy scriptures for the inspiration and instruction of us, his children. For members of The Church of Jesus Christ of Latter-day Saints, these holy scriptures consist of the Bible, the Book of Mormon, the Doctrine and Covenants, and the Pearl of Great Price.

Consideration of the marvelous way these scriptures came into being and have been protected throughout history provides proof that the Lord's hand has been ever-present in their preservation. He has made sure that his word, as written in the scriptures, would be maintained for our enlightenment and guidance.

The reality of this divine preservation can be seen particularly in the way the Book of Mormon records were obtained, written, and preserved. When Nephi and his three brothers were sent by their father, Lehi, back to Jerusalem to obtain the records that contained God's dealings with his children prior to their time, they encountered almost insurmountable difficulties. In the face of these obstacles, they were about to abandon the project. Nephi, however, inspired by the Lord, convinced his brothers that they must persevere. He knew that it was wisdom in God that they should obtain these records so that the teachings of the holy prophets, under the inspiration of the Lord, could be preserved for his generation and the generations to come. With the Lord's help, the records were obtained. The Nephite prophets added their own history to them, and the entire records were protected and preserved to come forth in these latter days for our benefit and use.

The Book of Mormon records were written and preserved by inspired men, many of whom did not know specifically why they kept them. Nephi, when he was instructed to make two sets of plates, stated: ". . . the Lord hath commanded me to make these plates for a wise purpose in him, which purpose I know not." (I Nephi 9:5.) This wise purpose was clearly described by a later Book of Mormon prophet, King Benjamin, who said, ". . . were it not for these . ... records and commandments, we must have suffered in ignorance, . . . not knowing the mysteries of God." (Mosiah 1:3.)

The great prophet Mormon, who was the custodian of all the records written and handed down by his ancestors, and who abridged and protected them, did so in full knowledge of their great importance. He knew that in so doing, he was following the instruction of the Lord. Mormon declared:

> . . . behold I, Mormon, began to be old . . . and having been commanded of the Lord that I should not suffer the records which had been handed down by our fathers, which were sacred, to fall into the hands of the Lamanites, (for the Lamanites would destroy them) therefore I made this record out of the plates of Nephi, and hid up in the Hill Cumorah all the records which had been entrusted to me by the hand of the Lord, save it were those few plates which I gave unto my son Moroni. (Mormon 6:6.)

Mormon's son Moroni also knew that the Book of Mormon records would be preserved for the instruction of future generations. He said, ". . . out of the earth shall they come, by the hand of the Lord, and none can stay it; and it shall come in a day when it shall be said that miracles are done away; and it shall come even as if one should speak from the dead." (Mormon 8:26.) Moroni also must have known that his words would come to us. He declared, "Behold, I speak unto you as if ye were present, and yet ye are not. But behold, Jesus Christ hath shown you unto me, and I know your doing." (Mormon 8:35.)

The Prophet Joseph Smith, in describing the Book of Mormon, said that it "was the most correct of any book on earth, and the keystone of our religion, and a man would get nearer to God by abiding by its precepts than by any other book."

The Bible is a collection of sixty-six books that describe God's dealings with mankind on the western hemisphere. This great scripture has come to us through many translations and much sacrifice on the part of many dedicated prophets, scholars, and historians. Certainly, our Father in heaven must have inspired and guided many conscientious individuals who kept the records and preserved them for our instruction.

President Heber J. Grant said, "All my life I have been finding additional evidences that the Bible is the book of books, and the Book of Mormon is the greatest witness for the truth of the Bible that has ever been published."[1]

The Pearl of Great Price, another of our standard scriptures, contains the writings and teachings of Moses and Abraham as revealed to the Prophet Joseph Smith and translated by him from ancient records.

The Doctrine and Covenants is our only truly modern scripture. It is a compilation of revelations given directly by the Lord to the Prophet Joseph Smith, with some additions by his successors in the Presidency of the Church. This wonderful collection of divine instruction is designed for our guidance in these latter days.

In respect to the Doctrine and Covenants, President Joseph Fielding Smith said, "The Book of Doctrine and Covenants contains some of the most glorious principles ever revealed to the world."[2]

Regarding all of the scriptures, President Wilford Woodruff said, "The Bible, the Book of Mormon, the Book of Doctrine and Covenants contain the words of eternal life unto this generation, and they will rise in judgment against those who reject them. All these records are words of God to man."[3]

The holy scriptures have been given by the Lord for our instruction. Yet, they cannot achieve their purpose to guide us throughout our lives unless we study them and put their teachings into action.

President George Albert Smith expressed this important truth in these words, "I admonish you, search the scriptures; read them in your homes, teach your families what the Lord hath said; . . . go to the fountain of truth and read the word of the Lord."[4]

---

[1]*Improvement Era*, Vol. 39 (1936), p. 660.
[2]*Conference Report*, October 1913, p. 9.
[3]*Journal of Discourses*, Vol. 22, p. 335.
[4]*Conference Report*, October 1917, p. 41.

By Love Serve
One Another

*And again I say unto you, let every man
esteem his brother as himself.* (D&C 38:25.)

A YOUNG girl was carrying a heavy
load in a basket on her back. Someone who met her along
the way inquired if the load was heavy and if she needed
help. As the young girl lowered the basket, she answered
with a smile, "No, it's not heavy. See inside—it's my
brother."

Most of our troubles and burdens in this life would
disappear if we could learn the fundamental gospel truth
that our neighbors and all mankind really are our brothers,
and if we could follow the Savior's admonition to love our
brothers as ourselves.

The difficulties, differences, and strife that all too often
arise in families, between neighbors, and among the nations
of the world develop because of our failure to recognize
and accept the principle of brotherhood. The central theme
of the Savior's message is the concept of brotherhood. He
knew that if we would but love one another, even as our
Father in heaven loves us, peace and goodwill would

flourish throughout the world. Paul, in his letter to the Galatians, expressed this thought when he said, ". . . by love serve one another. For all the law is fulfilled in one word, even in this; Thou shalt love thy neighbour as thyself." (Gal. 5:13-14.)

The concept of brotherhood is a basic gospel ideal. We believe that all men upon the earth are the literal children of our Father in heaven, and, as such, we are all brothers and sisters. If we could all attain and hold this concept and could learn to love one another, our serious problems would disappear and we would learn the true meaning of the Savior's statement, "Inasmuch as ye have done it unto one of the least of these my brethren, ye have done it unto me." (Matt. 25:40.)

Our Lord, in the Doctrine and Covenants' message (D&C 38:25), exhorts us to esteem our brothers. One who esteems another understands and respects him and holds him in high regard. The foundation of esteem and respect is understanding. It is an interesting fact that we are often suspicious and fearful of those we do not know. Acquaintanceship and understanding, however, can bring a knowledge and an appreciation of the virtues and good qualities they possess.

The story is told of two Arab boys who saw an object moving toward them over the horizon. Fearfully one said to the other, "It is a beast. Come, let us hide in this cave." As the object drew closer, the other boy exclaimed, "It is not a beast—it's a man and our enemy. Let us be prepared to fight." When the man drew close enough to be recognized, the boys both shouted joyfully, "He is not our enemy. He is our brother!"

If we would try diligently to get really acquainted with those we misunderstand or dislike, we would undoubtedly find that they possess many qualities that we could learn to esteem and respect. Jesus admonished us to love our enemies. Although this is extremely difficult to do, it brings satisfying rewards.

Fulton Oursler once said:

> *To love an enemy is a kind of exquisite common sense. Far from being naive or foolish, it is the height of enlightened selfishness whose wisdom nourishes the well-being of body, mind and spirit.*[1]

The spirit of the practice of brotherhood should begin in the home. If we make a conscientious effort to understand each other in the home and practice little acts of courtesy and kindness, we will set patterns that will reach out to our neighbors and to our brothers and sisters throughout the world. Paul, in his letter to the Ephesians, instructed his brethren, ". . . be ye kind one to another, tenderhearted, forgiving one another, even as God for Christ's sake hath forgiven you." (Eph. 4:32.) This, we should practice in our family relationships.

Our responsibility to esteem each other as brothers is effectively expressed and summarized in this verse, which has been set to music:

> *No man is an island, no man stands alone.*
> *Each man's joy is joy to me, each man's grief is my own.*
> *We need one another so I will defend*
> *Each man as my brother, each man as my friend.*[2]
> —*Joan Whitney and Alex Kramer*

---

[1]"Words to Live By," *This Week Magazine*, February 26, 1950.
[2]Used with permission of the authors, Joan Whitney and Alex Kramer.

Challenge Of A
Good Cause

. . . men should be anxiously engaged in a
good cause. . . . (D&C 58:27.)

ALTHOUGH history is full of dramatic
and world-shaping events, there probably never was a
period more critical and yet more challenging than the
present. There never was a time when the need was
greater for men to be "anxiously engaged in a good cause."

The word *anxious* means to be earnestly desirous,
to be zealous and eager. It implies particular concern for
both the present and the future.

If we strive earnestly and with determination to help
others, we are "anxiously engaged in a good cause."

More and more of our world's thoughtful observers
are now coming to the conclusion that the only permanent
solution to our heavy world problems lies in the area of
service, brotherhood, and genuine love for one another.

The Savior, who knew the solution to all mankind's
problems, expressed this basic thought when he said that
loving the Lord and our neighbor are the two commandments on which "hang all the law and the prophets."
(See Matt. 22:36-40.)

Many of us these days are asking ourselves how we can be anxiously engaged in a good cause and thus make our personal contribution in meeting the critical demands of the time. Some of us might be tempted to conclude that the little contribution we might make would be lost in the face of the enormity of the world's problems.

The answer to this was dramatically portrayed in an incident that occurred in New York City. Crowds in that city's subways were startled to see, along with advertisements for soaps and toothpaste, a car card displaying the Ten Commandments. The advertisement was signed, "Paid for by a friend."

In due course newspaper reporters, sensing the possibility of a story, tried to learn who this unusual advertiser might be. After considerable research and some difficult detective work, they learned that the friend was an ordinary stenographer. This was her personal project, motivated by the desire to influence others for good.

When she was interviewed, the stenographer said she had read someplace that "sometimes a small thing can change the world." To make this personal contribution, she had saved the cost of the advertisement, $400.00, from her personal earnings. Her contribution did much to focus attention on the Lord's commandments.

In our own search for a good cause in which we can be anxiously engaged, we need not seek such a dramatic method as described in the above experience. Our good cause may be service to others of a more personal, less publicized nature. We can be anxiously engaged in a good cause by sharing the saving truths of the gospel with our friends and neighbors; by seeking to lighten the loneliness, sorrow, and heartaches of those with whom we associate; and by encouraging and strengthening those who are down-hearted and discouraged.

It has been said, "The greatest of the world's heroes could not by any series of acts of heroism do as much real good as any individual living his whole life in seeking, from day to day, to make others happy."[1]

Let us, then, never allow the sun to set without making sure we have done some good, eased someone's burden, "cheered up the sad, and made someone feel glad." Let us always remember the words, "There are chances for work all around just now, opportunities right in our way. Do not let them pass by, saying, 'sometime I'll try,' but go and do something today."[2]

---

[1]William George Jordan, *Self-Control*, p. 191.
[2]*Hymns*, No. 58.

Concern For Our Neighbor

Every man seeking the interest of his neighbor. . . . (D&C 82:19.)

INTEREST in, concern for, and service to others form the foundation of the good Christian life. Throughout his ministry the Savior emphasized that the greatest joy and happiness come to those who center their lives on love and service to others. He said, "This is my commandment, That ye love one another, as I have loved you." (John 15:12.) Interest in, concern for, and service to others are the only genuine manifestations of true love.

One of the best known and most dramatic examples of concern for a neighbor is the Savior's story of the good Samaritan. Unlike others who had passed by the wounded man without helping him, the Samaritan bound up his wound, provided needed medicine, and took him to an inn for further care. His compassion prompted the Savior to ask the question, "Which now of these three, thinkest thou, was neighbour unto him?" (See Luke 10:30-37.)

Without doubt the best way to show our love to our

Father in heaven and to deserve his blessings is to love and
serve one another. The blessings that come to those who
love others and share their problem is expressed in this
poem:

> Each day we write with smiles or tears
> The history of the passing years:
> One's grief or joy another shares
> And life is sweet when someone cares.
> At last 'tis only love that lives
> And he who gets is he who gives.
> Who shares a neighbor's joy or strife
> Shall know sweet afterwhiles of life;
> Her songs shall reach beyond the stars
> Who shares our roses and our scars.[1]

Real joy, accomplishments, and personal success
come through selfless service. Someone has said, "Man becomes successful and great exactly in the degree to which
he works for the welfare of his fellowmen." The emphasis
in this thought is on work and deeds. Love without manifestation does not feed the heart any more than a locked
bread box feeds the body.

The importance of deeds rather than mere thoughts or
prayers on behalf of our neighbors is beautifully illustrated
in the following poem:

> I knelt to pray as day began
> And prayed, "O God bless every man."
> Lift from each weary heart some pain
> And let the sick be well again.
> And then I rose to meet the day
> And thoughtlessly went on my way;
> I took no steps to ease the load
> Of hard-pressed travelers on the road.
> I didn't even go to see
> The sick friend who lives next door to me.
> But then again when day was done
> I prayed, "O God, bless every one."
> But as I prayed a voice rang clear
> Instructing me to think and hear,

"Consult your own heart ere you pray:
What good have you performed today?
God's choices blessings are bestowed
On those who help him bear the load."
—Author unknown

In our modern, complex world we are growing more and more interdependent. As our lives become more specialized, we depend to an increasing extent upon the services performed by others. Consequently, we must take interest in each other. We need each other and need the assurance and feeling of security that come with being needed. We all hunger for the heartfelt and true concern of our friends and neighbors.

Manifesting a sincere interest in the welfare of others means more than giving worldly goods. When we have a real concern for another, we seek to build him up in his own eyes and to make him feel he is important and needed. We encourage him to noble endeavor and constantly assure him of our confidence in him and of our friendship. Someone has said, "There are more people in this world hungering for kindness, sympathy, comradeship, and love than are hungering for bread."

Let us resolve today to speak the kind word, write the note of appreciation, offer commendation for some worthy thing well done, and give recognition and approval to the efforts of others. Countless opportunities are present every day to show our neighbor that we have interest and concern for his well-being.

"I expect to pass through this world but once; any good thing therefore that I can do, or any kindness that I can show to my fellow-creature, let me do it now; let me not defer it or neglect it, for I shall not pass this way again." (Stephen Grellet.)

---

[1]Carrie B. Nichols, *Sunshine Magazine*, July, 1959.

Joy Of Service

Therefore, O ye that embark in the service of God, see that ye serve him with all your heart, might, mind and strength, that ye may stand blameless before God at the last day. (D&C 4:2.)

SERVICE is the foundation of a happy and abundant life. It is the cornerstone of the gospel of Jesus Christ.

This message from the Doctrine and Covenants gives new emphasis and significance to the meaning of service.

In it we are admonished to serve the Lord willingly and wholeheartedly. Service given stintingly, grudgingly, or in a boastful or prideful way is not acceptable. The Lord knows our motives, our capabilities, our weaknesses and shortcomings. He has given us the revelation from which this message is taken to help us overcome our shortcomings and in so doing to become more nearly perfect.

We can serve the Lord in many ways. We can serve him through working in the various organizations in the Church. If asked to work in this capacity, we should consider the call an opportunity, accept willingly, and perform our duties conscientiously.

Another form of service is missionary activity. This

calling too is a challenge and opportunity and one in which, if we are chosen, we should embark in all diligence.

The true essence of service to God, in these and in all activities, consists of service to our fellowmen. King Benjamin, as related in the Book of Mormon, said, ". . . when ye are in the service of your fellow beings ye are only in the service of your God." (Mosiah 2:17.)

During the Christmas season our thoughts naturally turn to that great area of service connected with the life of our Savior. Most of us are familiar with the story of "The Other Wise Man," by Henry van Dyke. This is the story of the Persian nobleman, Artaban, who, having learned of the birth of the Messiah, sold all his worldly possessions and bought three precious jewels. These he planned to take as gifts to the Messiah as tokens of his love and affection. Stopping to help someone in need, Artaban arrived late in Bethlehem and learned that Joseph and Mary, with the baby Jesus, had fled to safety. Artaban spent his life in search of the Messiah. In the process he ministered to the distress and suffering of his fellowmen. Three times he came close to seeing the Savior, but each time he found someone in need of his urgent help. One by one Artaban gave away his precious jewels in order to help others. He never was blessed with the opportunity of seeing Jesus and felt that he had failed in his mission. Yet, as he was dying, he heard a voice saying:

> For I was an hungred, and ye gave me meat: I was thirsty, and ye gave me drink: I was a stranger, and ye took me in:
> . . . Verily I say unto you, Inasmuch as ye have done it unto one of the least of these my brethren, ye have done it unto me. (Matt. 25:35, 40.)

Few of us may be called upon to give heroic service such as was given by Artaban. Yet, every day we encounter many opportunities to serve. To forget oneself in an effort to lighten another's burdens, to perform a thoughtful act, or to show an unexpected kindness is to serve the Lord by serving others.

If we are to serve the Lord with all our hearts, our actions, our thoughts, and our prayers must be centered on others. This thought is expressed in the following poem:

> *Lord, help me to live from day to day*
> *In such a self-forgetful way*
> *That even when I kneel to pray*
> *My prayer shall be of others.*
>
> *Others, Lord, yes, others.*
> *Let this my motto be.*
> *Help me to live for others*
> *That I may live for Thee.*

This type of human service does not require any special calling but can go far to help earn for us the promise of Jesus when he said: "Come, ye blessed of my Father, inherit the kingdom prepared for you from the foundation of the world." (Matt. 25:34.)

Heeding The Call
To Serve

*Yea, whosoever will thrust in his sickle and
reap, the same is called of God.* (D&C 14:4.)

THIS truth is of such significance
that it appears many times in the Doctrine and Covenants. Although the revelation seems to make special
reference to formal missionary activity in the Church, still
it has a message for every one of us. Although few of us
receive official missionary calls, each of us should consider
himself a missionary in the service of God.

The Lord has need of willing servants who have an
earnest desire to thrust in their sickles and reap, and when
he finds such a person, ". . . the same is called of God."
However, the message in the Doctrine and Covenants
(14:4) is not meant to be interpreted that anyone who has
the desire can, of his own will, assume authority and
responsibility in the Church. There needs to be order in
all things, and the Lord has clearly established the organization pattern through which he bestows his authority.

Those who hold formal positions and actively participate in church service must be called by the proper

authority. There are times, however, when some cannot hold a formal church position. For example, some are homebound; others have confining responsibilities. Still, all these can, if they have an earnest desire, share in the joy of thrusting in their sickles in the work of the Lord. They can make their influence felt as a tower of strength in the lives of those around them by setting lofty examples in their every word, thought, and deed.

One young mother, who longed to perform church service but who, while her children were young, found it difficult to participate actively in church work, received joy and satisfaction in performing various thoughtful and kind deeds. For example, she would take a loaf of newly baked bread to a homebound sister, or she would wash and iron the clothing of a sister who was ill.

Another Latter-day Saint sister who has been confined to her bed with a crippling illness for thirty years has learned how to thrust in her sickle. Although in pain most of the time, she has not let this torment affect her sunny disposition. Because of her cheerfulness, people more fortunate than she often seek her out to gain solace in their afflictions. Frequently, people cluster around her bed while she inspires them with words of wisdom and truth.

The Lord is aware of such service. Although these sisters are not called to official positions, still they are thrusting in their sickles in performing works of the Lord and, as such, they shall receive their rewards.

On the other hand, those of us who are able should accept any church position to which we are called. It is a rare privilege and an opportunity to hold a position in the Church. When we honor a church position and faithfully try to fill it to the best of our ability, we not only are helping in the Lord's work but we are reaping benefits ourselves. Talents freely used in the service of the Lord grow and multiply, and we become capable of rendering an even greater service. The Lord has promised us that if we heed the call to serve in his Church, we "shall be blessed both spiritually and temporally, and great shall be [our] reward." (D&C 14:11.)

Whether we actively participate in church work or render selfless personal service, the Lord extends to us an invitation to thrust in our sickles and reap. He who willingly and wholeheartedly accepts this invitation will reap rich satisfaction and abundant joy, and shall "treasure up for his soul everlasting salvation in the kindom of God." (D&C 14:3.)

"Unto The Least
Of These"

*For inasmuch as ye do it unto the least of
these, ye do it unto me.* (D&C 42:38.)

PROBABLY no other scripture has a more direct application to the responsibility we have to give service to others than does this quotation from the Doctrine and Covenants. The grand key words of the great Relief Society of The Church of Jesus Christ of Latter-day Saints are:

Said Jesus, "Ye shall do the work which ye see me do."

What was the work Jesus did? The scriptures testify that from the beginning to the end of his ministry, "he went about doing good." (See Acts 10:38.) The gospel teaches its followers to visit the sick, to comfort those who mourn, to encourage the downcast, to help the poor.

The doctrine of service to others as contained in this Doctrine and Covenants quotation was formerly given by the Savior when he taught his diciples on the Mount of Olives. There he described the events of the last days and said that when the Son of Man would come in his glory, he would judge his people and to the righteous he would say,

"For I was an hungred, and ye gave me meat: I was thirsty, and ye gave me drink: I was a stranger, and ye took me in . . . I was sick and ye visited me." Then the righteous would be puzzled and would wonder when they had done all these things for the Lord. And the Lord would answer them, saying: "Inasmuch as ye have done it unto one of the least of these my brethren, ye have done it unto me." (See Matt. 25:35-40.)

This doctrine of service to our fellowmen has permeated deeply into all religious and literary thought. Benjamin Franklin once said, "The most acceptable service to God is doing good to man." The great Book of Mormon king and prophet, Benjamin, expressed the thought beautifully when he said, ". . . when ye are in the service of your fellow beings, ye are only in the service of your God." (Mosiah 2:17.)

James Russell Lowell, in his well-known story of the vision of Sir Launfal, wrote these impressive words:

> *He gives only the worthless gold*
> *Who gives from a sense of duty.*
> *But he who gives but a slender mite,*
> *And gives to that which is out of sight,*
> *The hand cannot clasp the whole of his alms,*
> *The heart outstretches its eager palms. . . .*
> *Not what we give, but what we share,*
> *For the gift without the giver is bare;*
> *Who gives himself with his alms feeds three,*
> *Himself, his hungered neighbor, and me.*

A remarkable example of devoted service to others is found in the life of Dr. Albert Schweitzer, winner of the 1952 Nobel Peace Prize. Dr. Schweitzer's life was one of compassion, understanding, and kindness. From his youth he went out of his way to help the poor and underprivileged. While still in his twenties he achieved fame as a theology professor. He became a great organist and could have enjoyed a comfortable and properous life. Yet he was impelled to do even more for others. He became a medical doctor and established a jungle hospital for the natives of French Africa. There, like the Master whose life he tried to follow, he went about doing good.

Although our Father in heaven is all-powerful and can do all things, yet he follows the divine plan whereby his good works must be done through us his children. It is fine to pray for the welfare of the sick and the afflicted, but these are empty words unless they are accompanied by personal actions that help and comfort those in need. We can wish our neighbors well, but this is "as sounding brass or a tinkling cymbal" unless we do something that improves their welfare.

The Lord's divine plan requires that we go about doing good. If kindness is to prevail upon the earth, it cannot come about solely by wishing and praying for it. It will come only if we practice kindness and do good "even unto the least of these our brethren." A wise Book of Mormon prophet emphasized this fact when he said:

> . . . I would that ye should impart of your substance to the poor, every man according to that which he hath, such as feeding the hungry, clothing the naked, visiting the sick, and administering to their relief, both spiritually and temporally, according to their wants. (Mosiah 4:26.)

This is the substance of pure religion. This is what the Lord meant when he said: "For inasmuch as ye have done it unto the least of these . . . ye have done it unto me."

Serenity Of
The Soul

*Learn of me, and listen to my words; walk
in the meekness of my Spirit, and you shall
have peace in me.* (D&C 19:23.)

An ancient philosopher once said:
"Heap worldly gifts at the feet of foolish men. But on my
head pour only the sweet waters of serenity. Give me the
gifts of the untroubled mind."

Since the beginning of time, one of man's most serious
quests has been for serenity and for peace within his soul.

Men can win high honors and success; they can ac-
cumulate vast wealth and achieve great worldly conquests.
Still, if they fail to obtain the peace of the untroubled mind,
they can feel most inadequate and miserable. On the other
hand, men may have little wealth and never achieve world
acclaim nor honor; they may be robbed of their health
and caused to bear great afflictions. Yet, if they possess
the great gift of peace within their souls, they of all men
are most blessed.

One of our fine Latter-day Saint missionaries, at the
height of his effectiveness and shortly before he was to be
released, was seriously stricken with polio. For months he

lay in a hospital, fighting to regain his health. In an adjoining bed lay another young man who, while climbing toward unusual heights in a business career, was stricken with the same dread disease.

In one of their many conversations, our missionary inquired of the young businessman what he would seek to have if he were granted one wish in this life. The young businessman recognized the importance of the question and asked that he be given time to think it over. After a few hours he replied: "If you asked me that question a few months ago, my immediate answer would have been complete health. But now I can see that the most desirable thing in life is to have an inner peace and a spiritual serenity such as you exhibit. I long for that which you have, a constant awareness of the Lord's loving care. If, then, I were to be granted one wish, it would be for peace and tranquility within my soul."

Fortunately, not many of us must make such a sacrifice in order to learn the importance of the blessing of peace of mind. But all of us, either consciously or unconsciously, are searching for this tranquility of spirit.

In our quest for this peace, many of us are either trying to escape from the conditions of our environment or seeking for something we do not possess. In this search, some of us have persuaded ourselves that if we obtain certain worldly goods, we will find what we want. Others of us may think we can find this serenity by getting away from our environment and the things that trouble us. Whether through possession or escape, we hope to find a magic formula for peace, tranquility, and the untroubled mind.

The magic formula and the real answer to this most important search is clearly pointed out in the message in the Doctrine and Covenants (19:23) in which the Lord says:

Learn of me, and listen to my words; walk in the meekness of of my Spirit, and you shall have peace in me.

In order to learn of God, we must read and study the scriptures. One of the most beautiful poems ever written is the twenty-third Psalm. In it we read: ". . . I will fear no evil: for thou art with me. . . ." Fear is a natural enemy of peace. Throughout the scriptures we are told that faith and trust in the Lord will overcome fear. The Savior of the world said: "Peace I leave with you, my peace I give unto you. . . . Let not your heart be troubled, neither let it be afraid." (John 14:27.) One cannot read such words without sensing the elements of calmness and serenity.

Another requirement for peace of mind, as listed in the Doctrine and Covenants, is to "listen to my words." God's words are eternal and unchanging, and when they are spoken by the Lord's chosen prophets under inspiration, they are as if God spoke them himself. Let us listen to the words of these prophets, and if we listen to them we will heed their counsel.

The third commandment for inner peace is to "walk in the meekness of my Spirit." When we have learned really to know the Lord by reading of him and listening to his words, then we must put these words and teachings into practice in our lives. We must try to follow the example of Jesus and strive to become more humble, loving, gentle, kind, patient, and forgiving. Then shall we walk in the meekness of his Spirit.

These, then, are the requirements of inner peace as set down by our Father in heaven. It will take patient, conscientious effort on our part to fulfill these requirements. There is no shortcut we can follow, nor is there a magic lamp we can rub in order to gain our desired goal. But we will find the Lord ever willing and anxious to help us in our quest. If we diligently try to follow his counsel, we shall find that serenity and peace will come into our souls. Almost before we realize it, our quest will be ended, our goal reached, and the Lord's promise fulfilled:

And the peace of God, which passeth all understanding, shall keep your hearts and minds through Christ Jesus. (Phil. 4:7.)

Worth Of A
Soul

*Remember the worth of souls is great in
the sight of God.* (D&C 18:10.)

T<small>HIS</small> message expressed in the
Doctrine and Covenants, although brief, is profoundly significant. God's plan of salvation ultimately is concerned only
with the saving of our souls. Our Father in heaven said:
". . . this is my work and my glory—to bring to pass the
immortality and eternal life of man." (Moses 1:39.) Throughout all of his teachings, the Savior had the same great
goal in mind and expressed it over and over again in
exhorting his disciples to go into all the world and preach
the gospel and bring souls unto him.

This emphasis on the worth of souls is a source of
great encouragement. The Lord's declaration that the
worth of souls is great in his sight elevates mankind to a
level of dignity and majesty that should be a source of
inspiration and motivation to all of us. William Jordan expressed this thought in these words: "Man is never truly
great . . . until filled with knowledge of the majesty of
his possibility. He must first breathe the fresh, pure air of

recognition of his divine importance as an individual . . . as a great human soul with marvelous possibilities."[1]

Our Father in heaven organized the universe for the benefit of his children. All that this world is and all that it possesses is for us, to be used wisely for our joy and well-being. To fulfill its destiny and God's purpose, however, we his children must live so as to earn eternal life.

The great challenge this message brings us is how we can assist our Father in heaven in bringing souls unto him.

Our first responsibility is to make sure our own souls are saved. Fortunately, probably the best way to do this is to work conscientiously to help others save theirs. The joy of this labor is made clear in the following verse:

> And if it so be that you should labor all your days in crying repentance unto this people, and bring, save it be one soul unto me, how great shall be your joy with him in the kingdom of my Father! (D&C 18:15.)

One way all of us can help is to teach the principles of the gospel and bear testimony of its truthfulness to our family, neighbors, and friends. Too many of us overlook this wonderful opportunity to help bring souls to our Father in heaven.

Not long ago a mother presented to her teenage daughter a lovely antique silver bowl that her great-grandmother, over a hundred years earlier, had brought to Utah in a covered wagon. The mother told the daughter she hoped she would always cherish the bowl. She also suggested that when she was married and had a daughter of her own, she should in turn give the bowl to her daughter so that she, too, would remember the courage and fortitude of a great-great-grandmother who had forfeited most of her worldly possessions for the gospel. The mother said:

> Although this bowl is very beautiful, I should like to help you obtain something even more beautiful. I want you to possess

something more precious than silver or gold. It is something for which you yourself must work diligently. However, when once you have earned it, no one can ever take it from you, so long as you wish to keep it. This precious possession is a testimony of the truthfulness of the gospel. Your great-grandmother was the first in our family to possess this silver bowl and a testimony. This testimony had a profound influence upon her and also upon the life of her daughter, your grandmother. Now I, your mother, should like to pass my testimony on to you.

We can help also to bring souls unto our Father in in heaven through living exemplary lives. Consciously or unknowingly, we constantly influence the lives of those around us for good or evil. In order to make our influence felt as a power for good, we must have a firm and settled faith in the gospel and then must practice putting these gospel truths into action in our lives. We must so live that others will see the fruits of the gospel and will desire to follow its teachings.

Let us strive to bring souls to our Father in heaven. Let us always remember that "the worth of souls is great in the sight of God."

------

[1]William George Jordan, *Self-Control—Its Kingship and Majesty* (New York: Revell Co., 1905), p. 8.

As Ye Sow

Fear not to do good, my sons, for whatso-
ever ye sow, that shall ye also reap; there-
fore, if ye sow good ye shall also reap good
for your reward. (D&C 6:33.)

ONE of the firm realities of life
is that as we sow, so shall we reap. This thought has been
a central element of religious doctrine for thousands of
years. It is found not only in modern revelation but also
in the teachings of both the Old and the New Testaments.
For example, in Proverbs we read, ". . . to him that soweth
righteousness shall be a sure reward." (Prov. 11:18.) Paul,
writing to the Galatians, said, "Be not deceived; God is not
mocked: for whatsoever a man soweth, that shall he also
reap." (Gal. 6:7.)

A beautiful aspect of striving to do good is that in
the process we not only help others and perform useful
service, but in so doing we increase our own ability to
do more good. Step by step we tend to become that for
which we are striving. One good act performed makes the
next one that much easier. "For as he thinketh in his heart,
so is he. . . ." (Prov. 23:7.) Thus, we reap as we have sown.

The story is told of a little boy who, with his parents,

n oved into a house overlooking a deep ravine. One day, because of a reprimand, the little boy became angry with his mother. In order to give vent to his feelings, he ran to the edge of the ravine and shouted as loud as he could, "I hate you, I hate you." Almost immediately there came rumbling back at him an angry, hollow voice, "I hate you, I hate you."

The little boy was terrified, and running back to his mother, sobbed that there was a wicked man in the ravine who hated him and wanted to harm him. The wise mother took the little boy by the hand and led him back to the ravine. Then, in a tender, pleasant voice, she called, "I love you, I love you." A kind, happy voice echoed back the same sweet words she had spoken.

So it is in this life. Every good or evil deed we sow comes back to us in kind. We cannot wrong another without reaping an injury ourselves. And every good act we perform returns to bless us.

> . . . *Every good deed done to others is a great force that starts an unending pulsation through time and eternity. We may not know it, we may never hear a word of gratitude or of recognition, but it will all come back to us in some form as naturally, as perfectly, as inevitably, as echo answers to sound. Perhaps not as we expect it . . . but sometime, somehow, somewhere, it comes back. . . .*[1]

It is not only important to sow good deeds; kind words also have a reciprocal effect. As we sing in a well-known Latter-day Saint hymn, "Let us oft speak kind words to each other; kind words are sweet tones of the heart."

Ofttimes the most precious gift we can give to another is a word of sincere sympathy, love, and appreciation. Such words that express our gratitude to others spread cheer and encouragement. As wise Solomon said, "Pleasant words are as an honeycomb, sweet to the soul. . . ." (Prov. 16:24.) And in the words of our Savior:

. . . every idle word that men shall speak, they shall give account thereof in the day of judgment.

For by the words thou shalt be justified, and by thy words thou shalt be condemned. (Matt. 12:36-37.)

Let us, then, be conscious of our every thought, word, and deed and "not be weary in well doing: for in due season we shall reap, if we faint not." (Gal. 6:9.)

---

[1]William George Jordan, *The Power of Truth* (Deseret Book Co., 1934), p. 39.

Armor Of
Spirituality

*. . . take upon you my whole armor, that ye
be able to withstand the evil day. . . .*
(D&C 27:15.)

In GREEK mythology a well-known legend tells of the mighty warrior Achilles. In his infancy, Achilles' mother, Thetis, endeavoring to make him invulnerable to all physical harm, bathed him in the mighty river Styx. The water washed over his body, forming an impregnable shield with the exception of one small part—his heel. The princely warrior grew to manhood and, because of this protective armor, lived a charmed and secure life. Not one of his enemy's weapons could harm him. One day, however, after a great and successful battle, one last poisoned arrow was shot at Achilles. This arrow found its way to his one vulnerable spot, his heel. And because of this small flaw in his otherwise great armor, Achilles was slain.

In Doctrine and Covenants 27:15, Jesus admonishes us to "take upon you my whole armor, that ye may be able to withstand the evil day."

The emphasis in this quotation is on applying the whole armor of the gospel. It stresses the importance of building a strong protective shield of spirituality in order to resist the enticements of evil and the temptations of the adversary that are likely to beset us throughout our lives.

As in the legend of Achilles, most of us have potential or actual weaknesses in our spiritual armor that we must recognize and guard against. These weaknesses, although they may be relatively small, may open the door for seriously degenerating influences and may become an "Achilles heel" in our own lives. Some of these weaknesses might be selfishness, jealousy, intolerance, false pride, or covetousness. Even discouragement may be a flaw in an otherwise strong spiritual armor.

As Jesus exhorts us in the scriptures, we should gird ourselves with truth, make righteousness the breastplate of our armor, faith our shield, salvation our helmet, and the Lord's Spirit our defensive sword. (D&C 27:16-18.)

Let us be sure that we take upon us Christ's whole armor. Partial or incomplete righteousness will not give us the protection we need. Unless our spiritual armor is whole, Satan may find the weak spots. It is these flaws in our protective shield for which he is constantly searching.

With the complete protection of the Lord's Spirit and with his gospel, we can successfully withstand the temptings of the evil one and partake of the rich joys and blessings that come to those who stand faithful unto the end.

Continue In Steadfastness

> . . . *continue in steadfastness.* . . .
> (D&C 49:23.)

STEADFASTNESS is a character trait loved both by the Lord and by one's fellowmen. It is a synonym for dependability, faithfulness, firmness in the right. It means determination in adhering to sound principles. Those who are steadfast are unwavering in the face of temptations and obstacles.

Steadfastness is one of the primary essentials for accomplishment. Unless we have this quality, we are uncertain, easily swayed, and do not possess the perseverance to follow through to the end and accomplish those things we set out to do.

Steadfastness and conviction are closely interrelated. One cannot be steadfast unless he has strong conviction to which to adhere. Applied to the gospel, steadfastness means obtaining a strong conviction or an unwavering testimony of what is right and then having the courage and the willpower to live accordingly.

As we think about this important character trait, we

should remember that one can be stubborn in the wrong as well as steadfast in the right. Those of us who are stubborn and unteachable often develop a form of negative steadfastness that may be extremely harmful. For example, both Paul in the New Testament and Alma in the Book of Mormon, before they were converted to the truth, exhibited rigid steadfastness in persecuting the Saints and in obstructing the work of the Lord. Yet, both of these great prophets avoided stubbornness and were teachable so that when they were converted to the light and the truth they become even more steadfast and determined defenders of righteousness.

In building our own character qualities of steadfastness, we should examine carefully our convictions to make sure they are built on the sound foundation of what is right. Let us not be stubborn and unteachable. Rather, we should be steadfast in being good neighbors, in being kind and understanding, and in our service to others and to the Church. We should be steadfast in our good purposes, constant in the performance of duties, and faithful in keeping our promises.

On his birthday a loving father called the members of his family together to give them the benefit of his venerable wisdom. In respect to steadfastness, his counsel to his children was: "What means most to one when life is viewed from a long perspective is the assurance that one has never surrendered when the storms of life have beaten upon his face; that he has always stood steadfast for the right. . . . In the battle of life, the capacity to fight to the last rampart is the all-essential thing."[1]

Probably the most classic example of steadfastness in the face of adversity is found in the story of Job, as told in the Old Testament. Job was an upright and honest man who feared God and was greatly loved and blessed by him. Because of his righteousness, Job had prospered greatly in the land. Satan taunted the Lord and claimed that Job's righteousness was due only to the fact that the Lord had given him great wealth and possesions, and that if these were taken from him Job would lose faith and steadfastness. To test his servant, the Lord put everything that Job possessed in the hands of Satan. And one by one his possessions, his children, and even his health were taken from him. In the face of all this affliction, Job remained solidly steadfast. He did not waver in his own convictions nor in his faithfulness to the Lord. He staunchly maintained, "My lips shall not speak wickedness, nor my tongue utter deceit. . . . till I die I will not remove mine integrity from me. My righteousness I hold fast, and will not let it go. . . ." (Job 27:4-6.)

Job remained steadfast because he had an unfaltering testimony and immovable conviction. He knew that his Redeemer lived.

If we would build steadfastness into our lives, we must strengthen our convictions of what is right. On this foundation we will avoid uncertainty and wavering and will realize that "he that wavereth is like a wave of the sea driven by the wind and tossed." (James 1:6-7.)

Let us apply to our lives this message as found in D&C 49:23. Let us "continue in steadfastness" in being good neighbors, in being kind and understanding, and in giving devoted service to others and to the Church.

For our maximum happiness let us follow the counsel of the apostle Paul: ". . . be ye stedfast, unmoveable, always abounding in the work of the Lord. . . ." (1 Cor. 15:58.)

---

[1]Bryant S. Hinckley, *That Ye Might Have Joy* (Salt Lake City: Bookcraft, 1958), p. 32.

Magnifying Our Talents

. . . that every man may improve upon his talent, that every man may gain other talents, yea, even an hundred fold. . . ."
(D&C 82:18.)

O_{NE} of the misfortunes in life is the tendency of all of us to underestimate the talents and abilities with which we have been blessed. Most of us never realize nor develop more than a fraction of our potentialities. The reason is that we fail to use and improve upon the talents with which we have been blessed.

Utilizing our talents not only develops them, but also lays the foundation for the growth of additional talents. One of the great truths of life is that as we utilize, develop, and magnify our abilities, we gain the power and the strength to move on to higher and more important accomplishments. This thought from Ralph Waldo Emerson has been frequently emphasized as a truism, that as we continue in the performance of any task, that task becomes easier, not because its nature has changed, but because our ability to perform it has improved. In other words, there is no doubt about the truthfulness of the statement that "practice makes perfect."

The reality and accuracy of this message from the Doctrine and Covenants, that as we improve upon our talents we gain additional talents, was realistically demonstrated in the personal experience of a certain individual. This individual had received a beautiful patriarchal blessing. Among other things, this blessing stipulated that she possessed talents that she had not adequately developed.

As the years passed the only thing she could remember about her blessing was this statement, and she became increasingly more worried about her failure to develop her talents. In fact, she became convinced that actually, she was blessed with very few talents.

Nevertheless, as is characteristic in the Church, opportunities came to her to serve in various Church capacities. As she discharged each of these responsibilities to the best of her ability, she found that the accomplishment of each new task made her next assignment easier. Almost unknowingly she found she had developed talents of self-expression, leadership, organizational ability, and many others she had not realized she possessed.

This is the type of challenge open to all of us. Although we may not realize it, we have all been blessed with many talents. As opportunities for service come our way, we should grasp each one willingly and enthusiastically and perform each to the best of our ability. If we do so we will find ourselves developing additional abilities and, as promised in the Doctrine and Covenants, our talents will multiply, "even an hundred fold."

It is true that not all of us have great talents in some of the more glamorous areas, such as in music or in the arts. But all of us, by practice, can improve our talents of self-expression, of being better listeners, of having more understanding hearts, of being better husbands and wives, fathers and mothers, and neighbors. We can, if we conscientiously try, improve our sensitivity in seeing the good in ourselves and others, and in discovering beauty in the commonplace things of life. Through more pleasant attitudes, we can spread more sunshine and cheerfulness to those around us.

The Savior said, "For whosoever hath, to him shall be given, and he shall have more abundance: but whosoever hath not, from him shall be taken away even that he hath." (Matt. 13:12.) These words from the poem "Maud Muller," by John Greenleaf Whittier, are often quoted: "Of all sad words of tongue or pen, the saddest are these, 'It might have been.' "

As we contemplate the importance of developing and multiplying our talents, let us remember that our lives stretch into eternity, and the only things we can take with us are our talents and abilities and the characters we have built through the applications and experiences of this life. Certainly it behooves each of us to magnify and expand our God-given talents.

"Teach One Another"

"And I give unto you a commandment
that you shall teach one another the doctrine
of the kingdom." (D&C 88:77.)

T HE divine instruction to teach one
another lies at the foundation of the Church of Jesus Christ.
When Jesus was upon the earth, he spent his life in teaching others. After they had been taught, he instructed his
followers to go forth and teach one another. Yet, after his
crucifixion, his disciples apparently forgot the instructions
he had given them, and some of them returned to their
former occupation as fishermen.

Following his resurrection, to reemphasize their teaching responsibilities, the Savior called his disciples around
him and reinstructed them. In one of the dramatic events
recorded in the scriptures, he asked Peter if he loved him,
and when Peter responded in the affirmative, Jesus told
him three times to feed his lambs and sheep. (See John
21:15-17.) Then, before departing from his disciples, he
gave them his final instruction, which was to go forth and
teach all nations, "Teaching them to observe all things
whatsoever I have commanded you: and, lo, I am with you
alway, even unto the end of the world." (Matt. 28:20.)

Not only must we teach one another the "doctrine of the kingdom" through the Church organizations, but we also have a sacred obligation to teach each other in the home. We must make sure that our children have an understanding of the gospel truths.

On this subject the Lord has been very specific, telling us as parents that if we fail to teach our children in the home "the doctrine of repentance, faith in Christ the Son of the living God, and of baptism and the gift of the holy Ghost by the laying on of the hands, when eight years old, the sin be upon the heads of the parents." (D&C 68:25.) Moreover, we must teach our children "to pray, and to walk uprightly before the Lord." (D&C 68:28.)

Among the basic concepts of the gospel are the divine truths that "the glory of God is intelligence" (D&C 93:36), and "it is impossible for a man to be saved in ignorance" (D&C 131:6).

Knowledge, intelligence, and understanding are so important to happiness and success in this life. The teacher who imparts these to others is not only a fountain of joy, but he also earns the abiding love and gratitude of those he teaches.

Recently, in the classified section of a prominent newspaper, a notice appeared that attracted considerable attention. The paid-for notice merely stated, "Happiness is having a teacher like Mr. _____."

The notice was signed by the fifteen students of Mr. _____'s class.

An alert reporter, his curiosity aroused, sought out one of the students. He was told that all members of the class were so impressed and pleased with the sincere interest this teacher took in each of them that they decided as a group to show their appreciation by purchasing this space in the newspaper.

"Nobody wants this year to come to an end," summed up one of the students. "He's younger than most of us at heart," said another. "He makes our lessons live for us. "He loves us all, and we love him!"

When Mr. _____ was interviewed, he said, "Yes, I do sincerely love each of my students, and I am deeply interested in their individual potentials." Yet he believed that they had taught him more than he had taught them.

Without doubt the best way to gain knowledge and make it part of our lives is to study, learn, and apply, and then teach this knowledge to others. The apostle Paul said, "Thou therefore which teachest another, teachest thou not thyself?" (Rom. 2:21.)

President Brigham Young emphasized the same basic truth when he said:

> A man who wishes to receive light and knowledge, to increase in the faith of the Holy Gospel, and to grow in the knowledge of the truth as it is in Jesus Christ, will find that when he imparts knowledge to others he will also grow and increase . . . get knowledge and understanding by freely imparting it to others.[1]

The basic purpose of all religious teaching is to gain a better knowledge of God's commandments so we can put these truths into practice in our lives and thereby gain the blessings that come from living the gospel. Knowledge in and of itself is valueless unless it leads to constructive and worthwhile action. One has not really taught a gospel truth unless the learner's life through action has been improved. Milton expressed this thought beautifully when he said, "The end of all learning is to know God, and out of that knowledge to love and imitate him."

---

[1]Brigham Young, *Journal of Discourses*, Vol. 2, p. 167.

A Shield Against Temptation

Pray always that you enter not into tempta-
tion. . . . (D&C 61:39.)

ONE of the greatest blessings that
can come to us from our Father in heaven is the power
to discern and overcome temptation. In his struggle to
capture men's souls, Satan has no more powerful tool than
that of temptation. He knows that no man ever becomes
extremely wicked all at once. Sin, and the ultimate destruction that accompanies it, is a gradual and, often, a
relatively unobvious process.

President David O. McKay wisely said: "Temptation
often comes in the same quiet way. Perhaps yielding to it
may not be known by anyone save the individual and his
God, but if he does yield to it, he becomes to that extent
weakened and spotted with the evil of the world."[1] Recognizing this, our Father in heaven has provided us with a
shield against this subtle, but powerful, force of temptation. He has counseled us to "pray always that you enter
not into temptation."

In the Book of Mormon, Alma admonishes us to "call

on his holy name, and watch and pray continually, that ye may not be tempted above that which ye can bear." (Alma 13:28.)

Regardless of the nature of our faith or the strength of our testimonies, we are always subject to the pitfalls of temptation. This is why we have been counseled to so live as always to have around us the protective influence of the Lord's Spirit. This is what President J. Reuben Clark, Jr., meant when he said, "Build around yourselves an impregnable fortress of righteousness and depart not from your citadel."[2]

An Arab legend recounts that when Gabriel was depriving Lucifer of the weapons he needed to conquer men's souls, the wily tempter persuaded Gabriel to allow him to keep one device—the weapon of discouragement. He knew that with this weapon he could entice men into even grievous sins.

Recently, a young mother was beset with many troubles that seemed to move in upon her from all directions. When she sought counsel on how to bear these burdens, she was advised, "If you have trouble and Lucifer tempts you, pray to your Father in heaven and the dark clouds will disappear, and you will go on your way rejoicing." She was advised to pray constantly in her heart and to live for twenty-four hours as if Jesus were right beside her.

This she did, and she learned that when she approached each temptation and problem with the conviction that the Savior was by her side, her fears and discouragements vanished. She found she was able to control her temper, which so often before had controlled her. She was kinder and more understanding than she had been before. This was the effect of the Lord's Spirit and the fulfillment of the promise that the Lord gives to all of us that the presence of his Spirit will help us to avoid temptation.

This thought is beautifully expressed in the well-known hymn:

I need thee every hour, stay thou near by;
Temptations lose their power when thou art nigh.[3]

Prayer, then, is the real shield against temptation. Each of us should follow our Lord's counsel: "Pray that you enter not into temptation. . . ." (D&C 61:39.)

---

[1]*Conference Report*, October 1958, p. 92.
[2]Commencement Address at Brigham Young University, 1949.
[3]Latter-day Saints Hymns, No. 79.

A Testimony Of
Jesus The Christ

. . . and ye shall bear record of me, even
Jesus Christ, that I am the Son of the
living God. . . . (D&C 68:6.)

On one occasion when Jesus was
visiting a city known as Caesarea Philippi, in the north,
he asked his disciples who men said that he was. His
disciples answered that some believed he was John the
Baptist, some Elias, and others Jeremias or one of the
other ancient prophets. Then Jesus inquired of his disciples
who they thought he was. Simon Peter answered and said,
"Thou art the Christ, the Son of the living God." (Matt.
16:16.)

During his ministry upon this earth, the Savior knew
that if his teachings were to endure and to be effective in
the lives of his disciples, they must know, beyond the shadow
of a doubt, that he was the Christ, the long-promised
Messiah, the Son of the living God.

If this testimony was important when the Lord was
living and teaching upon the earth, it is even more important in our lives today. Not being blessed with the
personal presence of our Lord to counsel and guide us, we

must live by faith, knowing that his Spirit can be with us, if we seek it, and knowing that his teachings are not only the most effective but also the only genuine guide we have in this modern, complicated life.

When the impressive buildings that now constitute Rockefeller Center were built in the heart of New York City, a wise architect inscribed on the walls of the main building the following: "Man's ultimate destiny depends not on whether he can learn new lessons or make new discoveries, or new conquests, but upon his acceptance of the lessons taught him close upon 2,000 years ago."

Today we are experiencing earth-shaking developments and accomplishments in the sciences. We have created remarkable electronic devices that serve and entertain us. We are making marvelous progress in exploring the secrets of space, and men have even walked on the moon. Yet, none of these accomplishments or conquests will help us solve our basic human problems nor will they help us in any way to gain eternal salvation, unless we can bear record to the conviction that Jesus is the Christ, that he lived, died, and was resurrected for our salvation and exaltation. Only through this testimony and through a willingness to follow his teachings can we secure peace of mind, true happiness, peace upon this earth, and joy in the world to come.

Since the restoration of the gospel in these latter days, our Church leaders have borne countless personal testimonies to Christ's reality as the Son of God and have counseled us to strengthen and bear record of our own testimonies. As one example of these powerful testimonies from our Church leaders, President McKay bore this record: "With my whole soul I accept Jesus Christ as the Savior and Redeemer of mankind. Accepting him as my Redeemer, Savior, Lord, it is but logical that I accept this gospel as the plan of salvation, as the one perfect way to happiness and peace."[1]

President Joseph Fielding Smith, when sustained as the tenth President of the Church, added this testimony: "With all my heart I bear witness that Jesus Christ is the Son of the living God: that he called the Prophet Joseph Smith to stand at the head of this dispensation and to organize again on earth the Church and kingdom of God, and that the work in which we are engaged is true."

As members of his restored church we have a solemn obligation to build our individual testimonies and to bear record to ourselves and to others that Jesus lives, that he is the Son of the living God. How can we build this testimony?

Elder Marion G. Romney answers this question: "There are certain definite steps you have to take to get a testimony. You have to believe in Jesus Christ, that he is the Son of God. You have to repent of your sins. You have to be baptized by water and also by the imposition of hands for the Holy Ghost, and then you have to continue in obedience to the principles of the gospel."[2]

The best way to build and strengthen our testimonies is to read of Jesus in the scriptures, learn his teachings, and live them. We have been told repeatedly that if we do the things that the Lord tells us through the prompting of the Holy Ghost, we will know for a certainty that he is our Savior. Jesus said, "If any man will do his will, he shall know of the doctrine, whether it be of God, or whether I speak of myself." (John 7:17.)

We can also strengthen our testimonies both by listening to the testimonies of others and by bearing record ourselves. We should bear this record whenever it is appropriate, to our families, to our friends, and in testimony meetings. Moreover, when we partake of the sacrament worthily, and with singleness of heart, we bear solemn record to the Lord, to ourselves, and to those assembled that we "are willing to take upon [us] the name of thy

Son, and always remember him, and keep his commandments. . . ." When we partake of the sacrament, we should
concentrate on thoughts of the Savior and on the blessings our testimony of him brings us.

Through strengthening our testimony and bearing record of it we can say, with the ancient prophet Job, "I
know that my redeemer liveth." (Job 19:25.) As expressed
in the beautiful hymn, what joy and comfort this conviction brings. President Grant once said, "There is no joy
in the world that equals the joy of knowing in your heart
that God lives, that Jesus is the Christ."[3]

We are told in the Doctrine and Covenants that if
our testimonies and our lives bear record of our Savior
Jesus Christ, we have this promise of the Lord: ". . . do not
fear, for I the Lord am with you, and will stand by you."
(D&C 68:6.)

Surely no greater blessing can come to anyone.

---

[1]*The Instructor*, Vol. 99 (June 1957), p. 161.

[2]BYU Lecture, March 25, 1953.

[3]Albert L. Zobell, Jr., *Moments With the Prophets* (Salt Lake City: Deseret Book Co., 1960),
p. 197.

Blessed Is The Thankful Heart

And he who receiveth all things with thank-
fulness shall be made glorious. . . .
(D&C 78:19.)

T HE blessings associated with thank-
fulness are among those available to all of us. A thankful
heart is a gracious, joyous heart. Thankfulness is a frame
of mind. It is a point of view—an attitude that enriches
and gladdens those who possess it and warms the hearts of
those with whom it comes into contact.

The Lord has promised that those who receive all
things with thankfulness "shall be made glorious" and shall
receive blessings a hundredfold. This is undoubtedly due
to the marvelous effect that an attitude of thankfulness
has upon the individual who possesses it.

It is a truism that as we look for blessings, they seem
to magnify before our eyes, and we discover additional
reasons to be grateful. The attitude of thankfulness radiates friendliness, cheerfulness, love, humility, meekness,
and mercy. These are some of the character attributes
that the Savior found so desirable when he said those
possessed of them should be bounteously blessed and should
inherit the earth.

The Greek philosopher Plutarch wrote that "the worship most acceptable to God, comes from a thankful and cheerful heart." Isaak Walton suggested that "God has two dwellings; one in heaven, and the other in a meek and thankful heart."

A thankful heart is a priceless possession but one that is readily within the reach of all of us. Its possession is not dependent upon season, age, learning, or wealth. Like any other good habit, the attitude of thankfulness can be cultivated through regular and consistent practice.

If we will consistently express our gratitude on every possible occasion, we will find that an attitude of thankfulness will develop naturally. The simple practice of saying "thank you" and meaning it costs so little in time and effort and means much to those to whom it is expressed. If we want the rich blessings that come with thankfulness, we should develop the habit of expressing gratitude to our loved ones in the home, to our friends and associates, as well as to our Father in heaven for his many blessings to us.

Henry Ward Beecher portrayed the influence and contagion of thankfulness with this illustration: "If one should give me a dish of sand and tell me there were particles of iron in it, I might look for them with my eyes, and search for them with my clumsy fingers, and be unable to detect them; but let me take a magnet and sweep through it, and how it would draw to itself the almost invisible particles by the mere power of attraction.—The unthankful heart, like my finger in the sand, discovers no mercies; but let the thankful heart sweep the day, and as the magnet finds the iron, so it will find, in every hour, some heavenly blessings."[1]

If we would be worthy of the love of our Father in heaven, an essential aspect of our thankfulness must be our expression of gratitude to him for his countless blessings. All that we have—our lives, our talents, our health, the material things we enjoy, our assurance of salvation, and our hope for exaltation—are his gracious gifts to us.

The prophet Alma, in the Book of Mormon; admonished, "And now I would that ye should be humble, . . . asking for whatsoever things ye stand in need, both spiritual and temporal; always returning thanks unto God for whatsoever things ye do receive." (Alma 7:23.)

Thankfulness to our Father in heaven for his many blessings lays the foundation for the development of a thankful heart in all our relationships with one another. This is the key to abundant and glorious living.

---

[1]As quoted by Hugh B. Brown, *Continuing the Quest* (Salt Lake City: Deseret Book Co., 1961), p. 450.

The Glory Of Gratitude

*And ye must give thanks unto God . . . for
whatsoever blessing ye are blessed with.*
(D&C 46:32.)

On one occasion, when Jesus was
traveling to Jerusalem, he entered into a certain village
and "there met him men that were lepers, . . . and they
lifted up their voices, and said, Jesus, Master, have mercy
on us.

"And when he saw them, he said unto them, Go shew
yourselves unto the priests. And it came to pass, that, as
they went, they were cleansed.

"And one of them, when he saw that he was healed,
turned back, and with a loud voice glorified God,

"And fell down on his face at his feet, giving him
thanks:

"And Jesus answering said, Were there not ten
cleansed? But where are the nine?

"And he said unto him, Arise, go thy way: thy faith
hath made thee whole." (Luke 17:12-19.)

This account gives no details as to what happened to
the nine who failed to express their gratitude for the

wonderful blessing that had been bestowed upon them. The one grateful leper, however, was specially blessed and told to go his way, healed.

As we think about this incident, one fundamental fact should be remembered. Regardless of the nature of our blessings, the joy and satisfaction we obtain from them will never be complete unless we receive them with genuine thankfulness and gratitude.

The commandment that we must give thanks unto God for whatsoever blessings with which we are blessed is not given purely for the Lord's benefit. Our Father in heaven knows that our own enjoyment of blessings cannot be complete unless they are accompanied with sincere gratitude. In fact, we cannot be truly happy unless we carry a sense of thankfulness in our hearts for our many blessings. We must humbly recognize that all we possess comes from our ever-loving Father in heaven.

Thankfulness and gratitude are intimately related terms. President David O. McKay expressed this thought beautifully when he said, "Thankfulness is the beginning of gratitude; gratitude the completion of thankfulness."[1] To be sincere and genuine, both thankfulness and gratitude must involve more than mere words. They can only be demonstrated through concrete actions.

One way to express our gratitude to the Lord is by being kind to others. We can express our thanks by making sure that the "sunlight of our sympathy, tenderness, love, appreciation, influence, and kindness ever go out from us as a glow to brighten and hearten others."[2]

The importance of a thankful and grateful heart has been emphasized by wise men down through the ages. The great prophet Alma admonished the people that "every day they should give thanks to the Lord their God." (Mosiah 18:23.) Shakespeare expressed the importance of a thankful heart when he said, "O Lord who lends me life, lend me a heart replete with thankfulness." He also said, "God's goodness hath been great to thee.—Let never day or night unhallowed pass but still remember what the Lord hath done." George Herbert said, "Thou that hast given so much to us, give one thing more . . . a grateful heart."

Thankfulness for blessings received has been expressed by God-fearing peoples throughout the history of the world. The tradition of celebrating a thanksgiving day especially at harvest time dates back into antiquity. The American Pilgrims perpetuated the tradition in their thanksgiving ceremonies, which culminated in the establishing of Thanksgiving Day in the United States in 1863.

True thanksgiving is a constant thing. It cannot be confined to any one individual, time, or place, but should always be a part of our hearts. In true humility we should give thanks to our Father in heaven, from whom all blessings flow, remembering that just as we as parents appreciate an expression of gratitude from our children, how much more is gratitude due our Father in heaven. If we would please the Lord and find happiness within ourselves, we must follow his commandment and "give thanks unto God for whatsoever blessings ye are blessed with."

---

[1]*Pathways to Happiness* (Salt Lake City: Bookcraft), p. 317.
[2]William George Jordan, *Great Truths* (London, Hutchinson & Co., 1902), p. 26.

"In His Footsteps"

I will give unto you a pattern in all things. . . . (D&C 52:14.)

Tʜɪs statement in the Doctrine and covenants was given during a time when Satan was exerting great effort to destroy the organization and establishment of the Restored Church. As a result, many were being sorely tempted. So that they might not be deceived, the Lord assured them that he would give them a pattern in all things upon which they could model their lives.

One of the beautiful characteristics of the gospel of our Lord and Savior is that he requires nothing of us that he himself has not done. He has told us, "Behold I am the light; I have set an example for you." (3 Nephi 18:16.) Throughout his ministry, over and over again, he pleaded with his disciples and with us to "come, follow me."

Before he began preaching the gospel he was baptized, "to fulfill all righteousness." (Matt. 3:15.) This despite the fact that he was without sin. Knowing the extent to which we would be tempted during this life, he too set the pattern and submitted himself to the sorest temptations, in which Satan offered him food while he was hungry, great worldly powers, and immense riches. To all of these the Savior's reply was, "Get thee hence, Satan." (Matt. 4:10.)

During his ministry the Savior set the pattern in perfection, humility, love, faith, service, prayer, sacrifice, steadfastness, mercy, forgiveness, and all of the character traits that have come to be known as Christian virtues.

There are many beautiful passages in the scriptures in which these virtues are exemplified and taught. For example, "Be ye therefore perfect, even as your Father which is in heaven is perfect." (Matt. 5:48.)

In respect to perfection, we cannot hope to be as perfect in all things as our Father in heaven, yet this ideal must be attainable; otherwise he would not have so commanded us. We are approaching perfection as long as we are striving toward it. We can be perfect in many things in our lives—in paying an honest tithe, in fasting, and in many other ways. These are some of the details on which perfection is built.

In respect to prayer the Savior set the pattern: ". . . as I have prayed among you even so shall ye pray. . . ." (3 Nephi 18:16.) He instructed us to pray often, and gave us the Lord's Prayer as the ideal pattern.

On love, which was probably the central pattern of his life, the Savior said, "As the Father hath loved me, so have I loved you: continue ye in my love." (John 15:9.) The Lord said that our love should be all-comprehensive; not only should we love those who love us, but he also told us: "Love your enemies, bless them that curse you, do good to them that hate you. . . ." (Matt. 5:44.)

Every pattern of virtuous and purposeful living was exemplified and taught by the Savior. His gospel and the example he set have brought comfort and hope, strength and purpose to all who will accept and apply his teachings.

The pattern he set has caused countless individuals to live more Christ-like lives. For example, the story is told of a Christian missionary who was working with the natives of Africa. He told them about Jesus Christ and of the life of love and service he lived here upon the earth. One of the natives said, "He is not dead. I know him well." The missionary could not convince the native that Christ had lived long ago. The native insisted that he was still living in a neighboring village. When the missionary made further inquiries, he learned about a young man who had dedicated his life to helping the natives. He was caring for the sick, helping those who were poor, and in every way demonstrating in practice the Savior's teachings. He had tried to pattern his life on that of the Savior.

What comfort and strength, assurance and conviction the pattern of the Savior's gospel provides for us. If we will come and follow him, our lives will be opened wide for service, accomplishment, and happiness. The Book of Mormon prophet Moroni expressed the thought beautifully when he said:

> . . . I would commend you to seek this Jesus of whom the prophets and apostles have written, that the grace of God the Father, and also the Lord Jesus Christ, and the Holy Ghost, which beareth record of them, may be and abide in you forever. (Ether 12:41.)

The Savior and his gospel have set the pattern. Come —let us follow him.

The Good Shepherd

Wherefore, I am in your midst, and I am the good shepherd. . . . (D&C 50:44.)

Oɴᴇ of the most beautiful examples of poetry ever composed is found in the twenty-third Psalm, which begins with the immortal words: "The Lord is my shepherd; I shall not want."

This soul-stirring poem by the Prophet David has been, and likely will ever be, a source of comfort, inspiration, and uplifting guidance to most people. This is true not only because of the beauty of its inspirational language but because herein the Lord assures all of us that he is our Shepherd and that even though we may be required to "walk through the valley of the shadow of death," he is with us and his presence will sustain, comfort, and guide us.

What a wonderful, consoling, and motivating conviction!

If all of us could really believe with all our hearts that the Savior is in our midst and is constantly our Shepherd, what a blessed people we would be. How much peace, comfort, and assurance such a conviction would give us!

How diligently and conscientiously we should strive for this conviction!

Both anciently and in modern times, the Lord has literally pleaded with us to have faith that he is with us, ready, willing, and anxious to help and guide us if we will only live so as to build this conviction and to deserve his presence.

The blessedness of this comforting conviction was brought again into vivid focus sometime ago when a certain charming and talented woman passed away. She and her husband were a devoted couple whose many years of marriage had prospered on the foundation of love, understanding, and faithful adherence to the principles of the gospel. Her loving husband was deeply shocked and severely bereaved at her passing. Yet the positive assurance he possessed that the Lord was with him, and the Lord's promise through their temple marriage that they would be together throughout eternity, gave him rich solace, fortitude, and peace.

A very wealthy acquaintance, who a short time before had also lost his wife, sensing his friend's peaceful conviction, was so impressed that he declared he would give everything he owned in this world if he too could possess the same sustaining comfort.

Without doubt, the possession of a sublime faith in the Lord and in his constant presence is the safest anchorage of the soul. It brings peace and solace under all conditions. Someone has wisely said, "It is an inspiring thought that God is always present and accessible, that we can depend upon him with confident assurance at any moment of the day or night."

> Not alone as we reach for a star in the sky,
> Not alone as we live, not alone as we die,
> Let us never despair in whatever we do,
> Someone is there who will help us come through.
> We are left on our honor, but not on our own;
> Always remember—Man is not alone.[1]

"It is only reasonable that the power which made you, can and does sustain you. Listen much to God and he will instruct you and show you the way to go. In the degree of your meekness and obedience he will guide you towards light, truth, and perfection."[2]

During Jesus' ministry upon the earth he frequently emphasized the fact that he was the good Shepherd and that those who followed him were his sheep. On one occasion he said, "My sheep hear my voice, and I know them, . . . and they shall never perish, neither shall any man pluck them out of my hand." (John 10:27-28.)

Blessed indeed are those of us who always remember that the Lord is in our midst and that he is our good Shepherd; for if we build upon this rock we shall never fall.

---

[1]Copyright 1967 by Chappel & Co., Inc. Reprinted from *Guideposts*, October 1969, p. 3.

[2]Grenville Kluser, *Inspiration and Ideals* (New York: Funk and Wagnalls, 1917).

Time–A Precious Possession

. . . thou shalt not idle away thy time. . . .
(D&C 60:13.)

A_{LL} of us differ considerably in the nature and the amount of our physical possessions and in our abilities and talents. Yet, one precious possession in which we are all equal is the amount of time we have each day. Regardless of who or where we are, each of us each day has twenty-four hours of time—no more nor no less. What we do each day with this package of time determines the nature and accomplishments of our lives. Benjamin Franklin once asked, "Dost thou love life? Then do not squander time, for that is the stuff life is made of."

One of the most important lessons we can learn is to live each day as fully as possible without worrisome concern about what happened yesterday and what may happen tomorrow.

Constantly looking backward to what might have been lessens our faith in ourselves and injures our potential abilities. The past is forever closed. No worry, no agony of despair can alter it. As we are tempted to look to the misfortunes of the past, let us remember that when one door is closed, another always opens. If we busy ourselves looking at the closed door, we might easily fail to see the opportunities of the one that is open. The Lord has loaned us this golden moment of today to use to the greatest possible advantage.

Actually, we have only one day of life, and that one day is today. Yesterday has been lived and tomorrow may come, but today is here and now! This significant thought is effectively expressed in this well-known hymn:

> Today, while the sun shines, work with a will;
> Today, all your duties with patience fulfill;
> Today, seek for treasures better than gold;
> The peace and the joy that are found in the fold; . . .
> Today, today, work while you may.
> There is no tomorrow, but only today.[1]

This does not mean that we should not learn from our experiences of the past nor that we should fail to plan for the future. It is wisdom both to learn and to plan. But how well we plan for tomorrow depends upon what we do today. Today is the fruit of yesterday and the key to tomorrow.

It has been wisely said: "The most reckless spendthrift in the world is the one who squanders time. Money lost may be regained, houses and lands sold may be bought or built again. But what power can restore the moment that has passed, the day whose sun has set, the year that has been numbered with the ages gone? . . . We are spending time well when we are paying it out to God, to buy the things he means our lives to own, whether he is putting before us a duty to be done, a friend to be won, a small service to be rendered, a child to be consoled, or a house to be set in order. There is time enough given us to do all that God means us to do each day and to do it gloriously; yet, there is no moment given us to throw away."[2]

One of the great truths that the Church teaches in respect to our time in this life is its importance not only during this mortal existence, but also the significant role it plays as a fundamental part of eternity. Thoreau had a glimpse of this great truth when he said, "As if you could kill time without injuring eternity."

The great Book of Mormon prophet Amulek had a clear understanding of the importance of effective utilization of our time in this life as part of eternity. He said, ". . . this life is the time for men to prepare to meet God; yea, behold the day of this life is the day for men to perform their labors. . . . This day of life . . . is given us to prepare for eternity." (Alma 34:32-33.) If each of us would resolve each day to utilize his time most effectively, what great energy for good would be released!

We should not lose time in worry, discontent, and self-seeking, in useless regret, in idle and harmful activities. Life is for work and accomplishments and for the true joys and satisfactions that come therefrom.

Take time to work—It is the price of success.
Take time to think—It is the source of power.
Take time to read—It is the foundation of wisdom.
Take time to be friendly—It is the road to happiness.
Take time to worship—It is the highway to a better life.
Take time to laugh—It is music to the soul.
Take time to love and be loved—It is the end of all living.[3]

---

[1]Latter-day Saints Hymns, No. 215.
[2]Anna Brown Lindsay, *The Compact Treasury of Inspiration*, pp. 176-177.
[3]Albert L. Zobell, Jr., *Story Classics*, pp. 121-22.

"Doubt Not, Fear Not"

Look unto me in every thought; doubt not, fear not. (D&C 6:36.)

WE OVERCOME our fears and gain strength and peace of mind only when we place our complete trust in the Lord. David O. McKay, ninth President of The Church of Jesus Christ of Latter-day Saints, told about a group of Swiss botanists who were in the Alps collecting specimens of rare flowers. The group, he says,

> . . . started out one morning from a small village and after several hours' climb came to a precipice overlooking a green valley dotted with a peculiar flower, which, examined through field glasses, proved to be of unusual value. From the cliff on which the party was standing to the valley was a sheer drop of several hundred feet. To descend would be impossible, and to reach the valley from another approach would mean a waste of several hours.
>
> During the latter part of their climb a small boy had attached himself to the party and had watched with interest the maneuvers of the botanists. After discussing the situation for several minutes, one of the party turned to the boy and said, "Young fellow, if you will let us tie a rope around your waist and lower you over this cliff so that you can dig up one of those plants for us, we will give you five pounds."

The boy looked dazed for an instant then ran off, but within a short time he returned, bringing with him an old man, bent and gray, with hands gnarled and calloused by hard labor. Upon reaching the party of botanists, the boy said, "Sir, this is my dad. I'll go down in the valley if you let my dad hold the rope."[1]

The simple, unquestioning confidence this boy had in his father is the type of pure trust our Father in heaven hopes we, his children, will have in him. He knows that if we put our trust in him, we will keep his commandments and follow the paths he has laid out for our happiness here on the earth and for our eternal joy in the life to come.

This truth was beautifully expressed by Solomon when he said:

Trust in the Lord with all thine heart; and lean not unto thine own understanding.
In all thy ways acknowledge him, and he shall direct thy paths. (Prov. 3:5-6.)

A trust in the Lord gives us the inward strength and spiritual power to overcome life's temptations and to meet courageously its trials and sorrows. The human soul has great need for the sustaining strength that comes from the assurance that someone is near who can be depended upon. This is particularly true in family relationships. Every child needs the feeling of security that is present in a home where love, confidence, and trust abound. In a similar manner, all of us constantly need to be able to rely upon a Supreme Being for comfort and help. We need to be able to come to the Lord and unburden our souls and seek the solutions to our problems. In this way, we can gain spiritual strength and find peace of mind. Jesus, our Redeemer, has invited us to

Come unto me, all ye that labour and are heavy laden, and I will give you rest.
Take my yoke upon you, and learn of me; for I am meek and lowly in heart: and ye shall find rest unto your souls.
For my yoke is easy, and my burden is light. (Matt. 11:28-30.)

If we live each day the best we can, placing our complete trust in the Lord, we will have no need to fear, no need to regret, nor to worry, nor to doubt.

This important living truth is expressed in one of our favorite hymns:

> *Fear not, I am with thee, O be not dismayed,*
> *For I am thy God and will still give thee aid;*
> *I'll strengthen thee, help thee, and cause thee to stand,*
> *Upheld by my righteous, omnipotent hand.*
> *The soul that on Jesus hath leaned for repose,*
> *I will not, I cannot desert to his foes;*
> *That soul, though all hell should endeavor to shake,*
> *I'll never, no never, no never forsake!*[2]

---

[1]David O. McKay, *Cherished Experiences*, Clare Middlemiss, Comp. (Salt Lake City: Deseret Book Company, 1955), p. 190.
[2]Latter-day Saints Hymns, No. 66.

Earning The Lord's Trust

*. . . behold, you should not have feared man
more than God. . . .* (D&C 3:7.)

Recently a group of college students were discussing what they wanted most out of life. Some were seeking financial security; others, power; but the majority agreed that what was really important was the goodwill, respect, and approbation of their fellowmen.

It is good to seek the respect of others. However, we make a mistake when we allow our fear of criticism and disapproval of others to cause us to violate the principles we know to be right.

To fear man more than we fear God actually means that we are more anxious to please others than we are to live by the principles God has set down for us to follow and to earn his trust.

One example is in the matter of expressing thankfulness and asking the Lord's blessings in prayer. Sometimes in strange places or among strangers, many of us are tempted to avoid criticism from others, and we fail to pray.

The story is told of a young draftee in the army who had always knelt in prayer before going to bed. But in the barracks, in the presence of all the other boys, he feared to follow the usual practice lest he be ridiculed. Consequently, he waited until he thought all the boys were asleep before he slipped out of bed to say his prayers. On one occasion the young man on the cot next to his observed him and remarked that he, too, had wanted to say his prayers but had been afraid to do so. This gave both boys courage, and soon thereafter others saw them, admired them, and followed their example. Thus, nightly prayers came to be the regular practice by many of the boys.

It is true that often the very things we fear might bring ridicule from others actually build respect and admiration. Constancy, consistency, and adherence to right principles are choice character qualities. They are traits that all good people approve and esteem. Certainly those who fear the Lord and follow his teachings, regardless of the consequences, build strong characters and fine personalities.

To fear the Lord means that we have profound reverence for him; that we love and honor him; that our love is so strong that we will not knowingly offend him. When we fear the Lord, we want to please him by doing his will and keeping his commandments.

To those who have this type of fear and love in their hearts the Lord has said:

> I, the Lord, am merciful and gracious unto those who fear me, and delight to honor those who serve me in righteousness and in truth unto the end. (D&C 76:5.)

Yes, to seek to earn the respect and approbation of our fellowmen is good. However, if we are ever tempted to compromise our principles and ideals because of fear of criticism, let us remember:

> . . . it is better that a man should be judged of God than of man, for the judgments of God are always just, but the judgments of man are not always just. (Mosiah 29:12.)

Hunger For Truth

. . . ye must grow in grace and in the knowledge of the truth. (D&C 50:40.)

Mᴀɴʏ of us have been impressed with the fact that returned missionaries, in their home-coming talks, almost invariably state that the period spent in their missionary labors was the happiest in their lives. This is true regardless of whether their call took them into areas close to home or into far-off lands. Undoubtedly, a significant reason for this sense of happiness is because during the period of their missionary work they have been engaged exclusively in helping others and in serving the Lord. Another important reason, however, is because the period of a missionary's experience is usually a concentrated time of growth "in grace and in the knowledge of the truth."

It is a fact, all too often not fully realized, that happiness and growth in knowledge of truth are closely related. If we grow in useful knowledge, we develop our personalities and abilities and move forward toward the goal the Savior set for us when he said, "Be ye therefore perfect, even as your Father which is in heaven is perfect." (Matt. 5:48.) It is this type of progress that is the essence of genuine happiness and joy.

A divine example of the process of growth in grace and truth is that through which the Savior progressed. The scriptures tell us that "the child grew, and waxed strong in spirit, filled with wisdom: and the grace of God was upon him." (Luke 2:40.) When he was a boy of twelve his parents found him in the temple conversing with the wise men and astonishing them with his knowledge and understanding. All that the scriptures tell us about him from this time until the beginning of his ministry, at approximately thirty years of age, is that he "increased in wisdom and stature, and in favour with God and man." (Luke 2:52.)

The Savior himself, having grown in grace and truth, has set the example for all of us. Through his own experience he knows the great potentialities for joy and satisfaction that lie within the reach of all of us if we will make the effort to expand our knowledge of the truth. This is why he has given us the commandment that we must "grow—in grace and the knowledge of truth."

In the same section of the Doctrine and Covenants the Lord promises all of us that if we will seek after light and continue in God, we will receive more light, which will grow "brighter and brighter until the perfect day." (See D&C 50:24.)

Growth in truth and knowledge seems based on the same principles as growth in physical strength and power. We all know that if we allow a muscle to remain idle, it soon becomes weak and useless. On the other hand, exercise builds and develops strength. It is an absolute truism that the more knowledge of truth we acquire, the greater will be our capacity to grasp more and greater truth. Furthermore, it is a significant fact that the acquisition of one truth opens the door to many others.

Growth in truth and knowledge is a flowering process. As we travel up the road of knowledge, countless new paths open up to our vision, making our journey more and more interesting, beautiful, and challenging. James Russell Lowell wrote, "They must upward still, and onward, who would keep abreast of truth."

The Savior said, "Blessed are they which do hunger and thirst after righteousness: for they shall be filled." (Matt. 5:6.) He also urged us over and over again to seek after knowledge, promising that if we will do so, doors will be opened unto us and we will be blessed with understanding and wisdom.

Surely, we "must grow in grace and in the knowledge of the truth." This quotation from the Doctrine and Covenants has a special meaning for all of us. Regardless of how much we may think we know about truth, our cup really is never full. We must never stop learning if we would stay young and virile in mind and spirit. We must seek constantly to grow. If we do so, the Lord has promised that he will feed us from his ever-flowing fountain of truth.

Search For
Truth

For the word of the Lord is truth, and whatsoever is truth is light. . . . (D&C 84:45.)

Throughout the history of the world one of man's greatest quests has been in search of truth. Truth is the motive of the philosophers, the principal promoter of the poets, the compelling quest of the scientists, and the heart of all of man's religious yearnings. The world and all that is in it move forward on the foundation of truth. It is the unchangeable basis of all of life's existence and of its progress and development.

As emphasized in this quotation from the 84th section of the Doctrine and Covenants, the Savior came into the world to restore truth and light. He established his gospel to lighten our paths through this mortal existence so that we might have life everlasting and have it more abundantly. The Savior's life was the personification of light and truth. He said, "I am the light of the world: he that followeth me shall not walk in darkness, but shall have the light of life." (John 8:12.)

What is truth? Although this question has echoed

down through the ages, we are given the answer in modern
revelation: ". . . truth is knowledge of things as they are,
and as they were, and as they are to come." (D&C 93:24.)
One of our favorite hymns says:

> Yes, say, what is truth? 'Tis the brightest prize
> To which mortals or Gods can aspire;
> Go search in the depths where it glittering lies
> Or ascend in pursuit to the loftiest skies.
> 'Tis an aim for the noblest desire. . . .
> Though the heavens depart
> And the earth's fountain's burst,
> Truth, the sum of existence,
> Will weather the worst,
> Eternal, unchanged, evermore.[1]

Our most important endeavor in this life is to seek
and apply truth. A fundamental principle of the restored
gospel is that man is saved no faster than he gains knowledge. Wisdom and knowledge are derived from truth.
Truth brings progress. It is the foundation of happiness.
It is the only path that leads to the full growth and development of the human soul.

One of the encouraging facts about truth is that it
is all around us and is readily available to all of us who
sincerely seek it.

Many years ago during a bad storm a cargo ship was
driven far out of her course. She was badly disabled and in
helpless condition. The tide carried her into a strange bay.
The fresh water supply was soon exhausted on the ship
and the crew suffered the agony of thirst. They dared not
drink of the salt water in which they thought their vessel
floated.

Finally, in desperation, one of the sailors lowered a
bucket over the ship's side and against the pleadings of
his companions tasted the beverage they all thought was
sea water. To his great joy and amazement the water was

fresh, cool, and life-giving. The boat had actually drifted into the mouth of a great river, and fresh water was all around it. The sailors had simply to reach down and accept the new life and strength for which they had prayed.[2]

Like this life-giving water, truth is also all around us; If we are wise, like the thirsty sailors, we will reach out for the truth and make it part of our lives.

The Savior said, "And ye shall know the truth, and the truth shall make you free." (John 8:32.) To know the truth can make us free—free from sin, free from temptation, free from fear, and free to enjoy the glorious blessings and the full development of our talents and personalities. President Joseph F. Smith said, "If you will learn the truth, ye shall be made free from the errors of men and of crafts; you will be above suspicion and above wrong-doing of every description."[3]

In order to enjoy the rich blessings that come with truth, it must be applied and acted upon. Elder Richard L. Evans said, "There is no more virtue in the mere possession of truth than there is in the mere possession of food. Neither will save a man unless he uses it and uses it wisely."

Certainly, the word of the Lord is truth, and we, his children, should seek it constantly and apply it to our lives.

---

[1]Latter-day Saints Hymns, No. 143.
[2]William George Jordan, Self-Control, p. 71.
[3]Gospel Doctrine, p. 10.

What Is Wisdom?

Therefore, he that lacketh wisdom, let him ask of me, and I will give him liberally and upbraid him not. (D&C 42:68.)

SINCE the beginning of time, man's greatest need has been for wisdom. The progress of mankind has depended upon the wisdom applied in the solution of its great and small problems and decisions.

There has never been a period in history when actions and solutions, guided by wisdom, are more important than they are today. Man has made great progress in the acquisition of knowledge. Yet, with all of his knowledge, problems have mounted and multiplied until the decisions with which we are now faced are of such magnitude that, perhaps, our very existence depends upon their solution.

What is wisdom? The Prophet Job provides interesting insight into its meaning. He said, "Behold, the fear of the Lord, that is wisdom. . . ." (Job 28:28.) Solomon said, ". . . the Lord giveth wisdom. . . ." (Proverbs 2:6.) The first step in understanding the nature of wisdom is to recognize that it comes from the Lord and is available only to those who live his commandments.

The dictionary defines wisdom as the ability to judge soundly and deal sagaciously with facts as they relate to life and conduct. It involves intelligent discernment and judgment.

We should fully understand that knowledge in and of itself is not wisdom. Wisdom consists in the right use of knowledge. This implies that knowledge must be used righteously in full application of the teachings and commandments of the Lord.

How can we gain wisdom? Again, the scriptures give us the answer. In the Book of Mormon, the prophet Jacob declared:

> . . . *When they are learned they think they are wise, and they hearken not unto the counsel of God, for they set it aside, supposing they know of themselves, wherefore, their wisdom is foolishness.* . . . (2 Nephi 9:28.)

The apostle Paul, in writing to the Corinthians, said, "Not that we are sufficient of ourselves to think any thing as of ourselves; but our sufficiency is of God." (2 Cor. 3:5.)

To gain wisdom, then, we must gain knowledge on the foundation of spirituality and righteousness. This means that we must hearken to the counsel of the Lord. We must study and pray diligently, having faith that, if we work conscientiously, depending upon the Lord, he will add wisdom to our knowledge.

The most wonderful example of the application of the Doctrine and Covenants' message in respect to wisdom is the action taken and the marvelous results experienced by the Prophet Joseph Smith. He lacked wisdom on a most important subject. He wanted to know which of all the churches was the true one. Reading in the Bible in the Epistle of James, he discovered the passage similar to the one in the Doctrine and Covenants. The apostle James said:

If any of you lack wisdom, let him ask of God, that giveth to all men liberally, and upbraideth not; and it shall be given him. (James 1:5.)

We are all acquainted with the wonderful manifestation that resulted. This application of simple, pure faith was the starting point of the great and marvelous work that is the wonder of the world. These inspired words, put into action by Joseph Smith, gave him power to rise to heights of intelligence and wisdom and supplied him with the divine help that enabled him to serve as an instrument in the Lord's hands through which his church was restored.

The ancient King Solomon said:

Happy is the man that findeth wisdom, and the man that getteth understanding.

For the merchandise of it is better than the merchandise of silver, and the gain thereof than fine gold. (Proverbs 3:13-14.)

Each of us has a constant need for wisdom. Let us remember that it is an attribute of God, which he generously shares. However, each of us must first seek it with full faith that the Lord will give it liberally and "upbraid him not."

By Their
Works

For they shall be judged according to their works, and every man shall receive according to his own works. . . . (D&C 76:111.)

ONE of the most clearly established facts outlined in the scriptures is that men shall be judged by their works. Both ancient and modern scriptures are replete with statements supporting this fact. The Savior in his parables and in his sermons frequently stressed the importance of performing good works. He said, "Ye shall know them by their fruits" (Matt. 7:16), and emphasized the fact that "not every one that saith unto me, Lord, Lord, shall enter into the kingdom of heaven; but he that doeth the will of my Father. . ." (Matt. 7:21). Also, ". . . whosoever heareth these sayings of mine, and doeth them, I will liken him unto a wise man, which built his house upon a rock." (Matt. 7:24.)

The apostle James admonishes us, ". . . be ye doers of the word, and not hearers only, deceiving your own selves." (James 1:22.)

The prophet Nephi said that the day should come "that they must be judged of their works, yea, even the

works which were done by the temporal body. . . ."
(1 Nephi 15:32.)

The great King Benjamin instructed his people to believe in God and in his wisdom and power both in heaven and on earth, and warned them, "now, if you believe all these things see that ye do them." (Mosiah 4:10.)

This standard of "works" is one that has become a measure of an individual's worth, not only in religious matters but also in his attainments in every field of activity. We are judged by the skills we develop and apply, by our accomplishments and our attitudes, and by the extent and application of our wisdom.

A great pianist, amidst thunderous applause, had just finished his masterful rendition of an extremely difficult concerto. After the performance one of his admirers approached him, saying, "My, how wonderful! I would give my life to play as you do." To this the maestro replied, "Madam, so far that is exactly what I have given."

Regardless of the extent of our abilities, unless we work and develop them, we will never gain the highest achievement we may obtain. In this great church of the Lord's, we shall not be entitled to the love and respect of our friends and neighbors nor the blessings from our Father in heaven simply because of our knowledge or scholarship. Although knowledge and scholarship are important, they are useful only to the extent to which they are put to work in action in our lives.

In this message from the Doctrine and Covenants, the Lord said that "every man shall receive according to his own works." This means that we cannot expect to lean on someone else's abilities or upon another's testimony. We must work diligently and develop our own. We must have the courage and the wisdom to be ourselves and to rely on ourselves. In the final analysis this is the only basis upon which we shall be judged.

Someone has aptly said that no one can develop his

muscles by sending his servant to the gymnasium. In a like manner our Father in heaven will not recognize a proxy statement when we present ourselves before him. Only if our own works so justify will we hear that blessed welcome, "Well done, thou good and faithful servant . . . enter thou into the joy of thy Lord." (Matt. 25:21.)

Dignity Of Work

Cease to be idle. . . . (D&C 88:124.)

THE importance of industry and the evil of idleness are emphasized and reemphasized in the scriptures. For example, in Exodus the Lord tells us: "Six days shalt thou labour, and do all thy work." (Exod. 20:9.) In Proverbs, Solomon says, ". . . an idle soul shall suffer hunger." (Prov. 19:15.) And again, "Seest thou a man diligent in his business? he shall stand before kings. . . ." (Prov. 22:29.)

In the Doctrine and Covenants several passages warn us about the evils of idleness. For example, we read: "Let every man be diligent in all things. And the idler shall not have place in the church. . . ." (D&C 75:29.)

The opposite of idleness is industriousness. One who is industrious is steadily and perseveringly active. He is painstakingly busy and diligent and is devoted to lawful and useful labor.

There is a well-known story of an old farmer who, expecting to die, called his three sons around him and told

them that he was about to impart to them an important
secret. "My sons," he said, "a great treasure lies buried
in the land I am about to leave you. You must dig for it."

"Where can we find it?" the sons inquired, almost in
one breath.

"I will tell you on the morrow," the old man replied.

During the night the old farmer passed away. After
his burial, the sons began an organized project to locate
the hidden treasure. They set to work with spade and plow
to dig up and turn the soil of every foot of the farm.

The boys dug up no treasure, but they learned to work;
and when the fields were sown and the golden harvest
came, lo! the yield was prodigious, due to the thorough
tillage the land had received.

When he contemplated the harvest, the younger of the
lads observed, "I think I know what father meant when he
said that a treasure lay hidden in the fields, but we would
have to dig for it."

We should all be eternally grateful for the blessings
of work and for the development that purposeful industry
brings to each of us. Charles Kingsley has said, "Thank God
every morning when you get up that you have something
to do that day which must be done, whether you like it
or not. Being forced to work, and forced to do your best,
will breed in you temperance and self-control, diligence
and strength of will, cheerfulness and content, and a hundred virtues which the idle never know."[1]

Without doubt the most effective medicine to heal
discontent and drive away discouragement is purposeful
and diligent work.

Most of us have within us the necessary power for
useful, progressive, and successful lives. If, through purposeful work, we apply the abilities that may lie dormant within us, our powers for accomplishment will develop and
grow.

We are now living during a period of remarkable opportunities, when the Lord has poured out his Spirit upon the inhabitants of the earth. It is a glorious and choice opportunity for each of us to be a part of this great progress, and to be able, through industry and work, to make our small but most important contribution.

For our own happiness and success, we should heed this commandment of the Lord as stated in the Doctrine and Covenants. We must not fritter away our time in useless, idle, and unimportant pursuits. If we are industrious we will aspire, plan, organize, concentrate, use our initiative, analyze, and accomplish. These are the ingredients of constructive work and the tools of satisfying success.

> *Let us, then, be up and doing,*
> *With a heart for any fate;*
> *Still achieving, still pursuing,*
> *Learn to labor and to wait.*[2]

---

[1]Ezra L. Marler, *Golden Nuggets of Thought*, Vol. 2, p. 148.
[2]Henry Wadsworth Longfellow, "Song of Life."

Labor's Rich
Reward

*. . . I will bless all those who labor in my
vineyard with a mighty blessing. . . .*
(D&C 21:9.)

WORKING in the Lord's vineyard
is one of life's choice experiences. This work brings rich
blessings both to those who do the work and to those who
benefit by the labor. The promise contained in this message
in the Doctrine and Covenants (21:9) emphasizes the fact
that a mighty blessing comes to those who perform the
work. To qualify for these blessings, it is important that
we understand what the Lord means when he refers to
laboring in his vineyard, and what blessings may be expected from this promise.

The term labor in the sense given in the quotation
signifies action. It means efficient expenditure of time
and energy in useful service for others. When we labor,
we do not spend our time in passive well-wishing. We back
up our well-wishing with well-doing. We substitute concrete deeds for good intentions.

Jesus and his apostles repeatedly emphasized the fact
that the gospel is one of work and service. To gain blessings,

we must be "doers of the word, and not hearers only. . . ." (James 1:22.)

The Lord's vineyard is defined as a field of "spiritual endeavor." When we are actively engaged in selfless service to others, we are helping to build the Lord's kingdom on earth and, as such, are working in life's most important spiritual endeavor.

We can labor in the Lord's vineyard in various ways. One way is to accept willingly and humbly any calling requested of us in the Church. Church work fundamentally involves service to others. It is one of the most direct ways of laboring in the Lord's vineyard.

However, there are many other ways not directly connected with church assignments in which one can perform this service. One of the most blessed of these is that unselfish human service which springs from the heart and consists of doing all we can to help ease others' burdens and to try to bring happiness into their lives. This labor consists in following the admonition of James: ". . .To visit the fatherless and widows in their affliction. . . ." (James 1:27.) It involves giving willingly and freely of ourselves, without any thought of reward, honor, or glory. James Russell Lowell beautifully expressed this thought in his "Vision of Sir Launfal":

> Not what we give, but what we share,
> For the gift without the giver is bare;
> Who gives himself, with his alms feeds three,
> Himself, his hungering neighbor, and me.

One of the great truths associated with service performed for others is that enduring and richly satisfying blessings are showered upon the giver. A prominent church man tells of the occasion when he was bedfast for several weeks. During this period a busy friend, active in business and civic affairs, visited him regularly once each week and spent an hour reading to him from an inspirational book.

These friendly visits gave the man who was ill something concrete and uplifting to look forward to and did much to raise his spirits and help restore him more quickly to full health. The bedridden friend never forgot those kind acts. Years later, when he was again expressing his appreciation for them, the visitor remarked that he was the one who had been really blessed. He said:

> At that time I was going through a particularly trying period in my business. The book which I read to you gave much needed repose and refreshment to my soul. When I returned to my business, after those visits, I was able to think more clearly and to approach my work with renewed vigor. Problems seemed to melt away and I felt an inner sense of contentment and happiness which sustained me through the week. I was the one who was truly blessed.

To bless, according to one definition, means to make happy, to guard, keep, and protect. One of the Lord's mighty blessings, then, means to bestow great and lasting happiness. It means that the Lord will encircle us with his secure, protecting care. He will grant us contentment and peace of mind. This mighty blessing is the inevitable reward of those who hearken to the Savior's teachings and who do his will by losing themselves in the service of others. The Savior has said: ". . . he who doeth the works of righteousness shall receive his reward. . . ." (D&C 59:23.) What a choice reward it is to have the true, soul-satisfying happiness that comes when we diligently and wholeheartedly labor in the Lord's vineyard.

"Look To This Day"

Wherefore, if ye believe me, ye will labor while it is called today. (D&C 64:25.)

Pᴇᴏᴘʟᴇ of action—those who get things done—are invariably individuals who have fixed and settled beliefs and definite goals. These people are dedicated, devoted, and determined, because of unwavering convictions of the importance and necessity of that which they are doing.

When the Lord said, as recorded in the D&C 64:25, "Wherefore, if ye believe me, ye will labor while it is called today," he was emphasizing two important, closely related facts. First, genuine belief is the motivator of action. Unless we have strong convictions, we are likely to postpone actions and not do those things which we should do at the time they should be done. The Savior said, "He that believeth on me, the works that I do shall he do also." (John 14:12.) Belief, then, is the important essential. If we would follow the Lord's counsel, we will do all of the things he has commanded us because believing, we will know that by following his counsel and commandments we can find joy and happiness in this life. The second fact emphasized in this scripture is that if we truly believe the Lord, we will labor (act) *today*—not in some indefinite future.

One of the most important things to remember about action is that it is "no action" until it is taken—until something is done. In other words, postponed, procrastinated, and just dreamed-about action is no action.

The trouble with postponing until tomorrow the things we should do today is that tomorrow may be too late. In fact, tomorrow really never comes. Life is made up of a succession of todays.

Someone has said, "Every day is a new life to a wise man." Thomas Carlyle expressed the thought this way when he said, "Our main business is not to see what lies dimly at a distance, but to do what lies clearly at hand."

The importance of laboring today is expressed beautifully by the Indian dramatist Kalidasa:

> *Look to this day*
> *For it is life, the very life of life.*
> *In its brief course*
> *Lie all the verities and realities of your existence;*
> *Yesterday is but a dream*
> *And tomorrow is only a vision,*
> *But today well lived makes every yesterday a dream of happiness*
> *And every tomorrow a vision of hope.*
> *Look well, therefore, to this day!*

The ancient psalmist also advises us, "This is the day which the Lord hath made; we will rejoice and be glad in it." (Ps. 118:24).

Our application of these thoughts consists in strengthening our beliefs so that they become real motivators of action. Let us ask ourselves, do we really have faith that Jesus is our Lord and Savior? Do we really have faith in his teachings? If we do, we will do the things he has told us to do.

We will *today* perform those little acts of neighborly kindnesses which should be done today, but which we so often postpone. We will *today* overcome those little personal weaknesses and habits which we are always going to overcome but which we never quite seem to accomplish. We will *today* express gratitude and appreciation for those deeds of kindness and thoughtfulness performed to us and for us by others.

In the Book of Mormon, the prophet Samuel the Lamanite told of the predicament in which the people of his time found themselves because they had procrastinated the day of their salvation until it was too late. They had sought happiness too much in worldly material things and had failed each day, through postponement, to overcome and repent of their weaknesses and imperfections. They had failed to perform those acts of kindness which are the essence of the Savior's teachings. Samuel told the people that their days of probation were past and their exaltation lost because of their procrastination. (See Helaman 13.)

Surely the counsel given to us in Doctrine and Covenants 64:25 is both timely and pertinent. *Today* is the day of our salvation. If we are truly wise we will heed the Lord and believe him, and do the things he instructs us while it is yet today.

Persistence In Well-doing

Wherefore, be not weary in well-doing. . . .
(D&C 64:33.)

Wʜᴇɴ the Lord gave the instruction "Be not weary in well-doing," he emphasized the fact that great accomplishments come out of doing small things well. In the same verse in the Doctrine and Covenants, he said, ". . . out of small things proceedeth that which is great." As we admire and applaud the honors which come to certain individuals as a result of their great accomplishments, we are prone to overlook the fact that these outstanding achievements have come only as a result of their having done well a great number of small and often tedious routine things. This is true of a priceless piece of art, of a fine symphony, or of a beautiful building. Only when minute care is given to the small details can the finished product be great.

The story is told that when Michelangelo was working on one of his great masterpieces, a friend called and observed him at his work. Some weeks later this friend visited the master artist again, but could see very little change in the painting. When he commented on this, Michelangelo pointed out that he had changed slightly the expression of the eyes, had added a little color here, and had changed a line there. "But these are small details," the friend replied.

"Yes," the artist responded, "but perfection is composed of details, but perfection is no detail."

In avoiding "weariness in well-doing," we should recognize the joy that comes from doing well the little, good things. It is a truism that no one can really accomplish great things without being good, and most frequently true goodness springs from the simple little things.

Recently a newspaper published an editorial praising the life of an outstanding woman who had passed away. The editorial emphasized the fact that her life had been beautifully meaningful, because in many little ways she had brought inspiration and encouragement to others. She had consistently put service above any consideration of personal comfort or convenience. Over a long period of years, on a firm, self-imposed schedule, she had frequently visited the ill and shut-ins. On a birthday in her late eighties she acknowledged the gift of a box of candy, saying, "This is wonderful. I'll take it to some of the old folks I'm visiting." Most of these "old folks" were younger than she. This is the type of selfless, dedicated "well-doing" which distinguishes a life and makes it great.

Someone has said that the requisite for great living is the ability to do common things uncommonly well. All of us can wisely profit by applying to our lives the divine instruction of not wearying in well-doing.

James Allen, in his little book *The Heavenly Life,* sums up this thought with these lines: "Lay up each year thy harvest of well-doing, wealth that kings nor thieves can take away. When all the things thou callest thine, goods, pleasures, honors fall; thou in thy virtue shall survive them all."[1]

Let us follow the admonition of the Lord when he said,

"Wherefore, be not weary in well-doing," recognizing the fact that "out of small things proceedeth that which is great."

---

[1]James Allen, *The Heavenly Life* (New York: H. M. Caldwell Co.), p. 39.

INDEX

A

Achilles, 173
Adversity, 1-4
Affliction, 1-4
Agents unto themselves, 18-20
Allen, James, 234
Anxiously engaged, 149
Apostles, 22
Architect, story about, 21
Armor, 173-74
Atonement, 60

B

Bailey, Temple, 38
Beauty, 71-73
Beecher, Henry Ward, 192
Bible, 144-45
Blessings, 229
Bondage, 56-57
Book of Mormon, 142-45
Brotherhood, 146-48
Brown, Hugh B., 39, 58, 121
Burdens, 2, 146

C

Calmness, 107
Cannon, George Q., 20
Carlyle, Thomas, 231
Cavell, Edith, 52
Character, 5-7, 209-10
Charity, 8-11, 94
Cheerfulness, 12-14, 72
"Child Learns What He Lives," 16
Children, 15-17, 182, 207
Christmas, 60, 62
Church callings, 158-60
Citizenship, 91
Clark, J. Reuben, Jr., 88, 185
Clayton, William R., 108
Commandments, 18-26, 35, 92-94
Communication, 61, 116
Communism, 55
Confidence, 19
Confucius, 52
Conscience, 59, 76
Contrite spirit, 122-24
Convictions, 230
Cornelia, 15

Council in heaven, 54
Counsel the Lord, 66
Croft, Roy, 96

D

DeMille, Cecil B., 25
Details, 234
Dignity, 79
Diogenes, 75
Discipleship, 27-29
Discouragement, 185
Doctrine and Covenants, vii-ix 144-45
Doers of the word, 22

E

Elisha, 104
Emerson, Ralph Waldo, 110, 178
Endurance, 34-36
Enemies, 52
"Essay on Man," 59
Evans, Richard L., 217
Evil, 30-33, 138
Exaltation, 21
Example, 16-17, 197, 199
Experience, 17, 114

F

Faith, 34-46, 64, 201
Faithful preserved, 37-39
Family, 69-73
Faultfinding, 47-50, 88
Fear, 166, 206, 209
Feathers, 30
First principle, 44
Fishermen, story about, 22
Fog, story about, 111
Forget, 52
Forgiveness, 51-53, 131
Franklin, Benjamin, 162, 203
Free agency, 18-20, 54-56, 58, 60, 84
Freedom, 54, 57-59, 217
Friendliness, 65

G

General Board of Relief Society, v
General Relief Society Presidency, ix
Gentleness, 107
Gibran, Kahlil, 10-11
Gifts, 60-65

Goethe, Johann, 1
Good cause, 149-51
Good Samaritan, 100, 152
Gossip, 30-33
Grace, 72-73
Grant, Heber J., viii, 35, 110, 117, 144, 190
Gratitude, 194-96
Growth, 212-14
Guidance, 66-68

H

Hamlet, 117
Heavenly Life, The, 234
Herbert, George, 196
Home, 69-73, 182
Honesty, 74-77
Humility, 78-81

I

Idleness, 82-85, 224
Initiative, 18-19
Integrity, 74-77

J

Job, 134-35, 176
Jordan, William George, 167
Judgment, 18-19, 86-89
Justice, 86-89

K

Kalidasa, 231
Keller, Helen, 98
Kingsley, Charles, 225
Knowledge, 110, 181-83, 216, 219, 222
Kramer, Alex, 148

L

Labor, 227
Law, 27, 57, 103-5
Law, Dorothy L., 16
Long-suffering, 107
Lord's vineyard, 227-29
Love, 17, 24, 90-96, 105, 147-49, 198
"Love," 95-96
Lowell, James Russell, 162, 214, 228

M

Magnet, story about, 192
"Mansion, the," 10
"Maud Muller," 180

Meekness, 97-99
Merchant of Venice, 101
Mercy, 100-102
Michelangelo, 233
Milton, John, 133, 183
Missionaries, 158-59, 212
Moore, Thomas, 2
Mortality, 205
Morte D'Arthur, 127
Mother, story about, 38
Moyle, Henry D., 19
McKay, David O., 47, 55, 86, 125, 184, 188, 195, 206

N

Naaman, 104
Neighbors, 32, 152-54
Nobility, 80

O

Obedience, 24-26, 67, 91, 103-5
"Other Wise Man, the," 156
Oursler, Fulton, 148

P

Parable of talents, 61
Parenthood, 69
Patience, 106-8
Patriarchal blessing, story about, 179
Peace, 59, 164-66
Pearl of Great Price, 144-45
Perfection, 106, 198
Perseverance, 107-8
Persistence, 110-11, 233-35
Pilot, story about, 58
Plato, 19
Plutarch, 192
Pope, Alexander, 59, 74
Power, 109-11
Prayer, 17, 66-68, 112-27, 184-86, 198, 210
Pride, 128-30
Procrastination, 231-32

R

Reaping, 170-72
Relief Society, 8, 32, 101-2, 161
Relief Society Magazine, v, ix
Relief Society visiting teachers messages, v, ix
Repentance, 131-33
Resentment, 52

Respect, 209-11
Righteousness, 57, 134-37
Rockefeller Center, story about, 188
Romney, Marion G., 67, 189

S

Sacrament, 189-90
Satan, 138-41
Saving souls, 167-69
Savior, 197-202
Schweitzer, Albert, 162
Scriptures, 24, 142-45
Sculptor, story about, 101
Seek, 119-21
Self-control, 107
Self-reliance, 19
Serenity, 164-66
Service, 146-63, 234
Shakespeare, William, 76, 101, 117, 195
Sharpe, R. L., 7
Shepherd, 200-202
Sin, 57, 131-33
Smith, George Albert, 137, 145
Smith, Joseph, vi, 8, 18, 30, 32, 64, 95, 102, 114, 144, 219-20
Smith, Joseph F., 132, 145
Smith, Joseph Fielding, 145, 189
Socrates, 82
Soul, 164-69
Sowing, 170-72
Spafford, Belle S., vi
Spirituality, 173-74
Stagecoach, story about, 140
Steadfastness, 37-39, 97-99, 175-77
Strength, 80-81
Stubbornness, 176
Sullivan, Ann (Macy), 98

T

Talents, 60-62, 85, 178-80
Teaching, 16, 69, 181-83
Temptation, 34, 138-41, 184-86
Ten Commandments, 25, 58, 150
Tennyson, Alfred Lord, 127
Testimony, 6, 169, 187-90
Thankfulness, 191-96
Thoreau, Henry David, 205
Time, 84, 203-5
Today, 230-32
Trees, story about, 35-36
Trust, 74, 206-11
Truth, 212-17
"Truths to Live By From the Doctrine and Covenants," ix

U

Unprofitable servants, 18-19

V

Van Dyke, Henry, 10, 156
"Vision of Sir Launfal," 162, 228
Voices of warning, 22

W

Walton, Isaak, 192
Well-doing, 233-35
Whitney, Joan, 148
Whittier, John Greenleaf, 180
Widtsoe, John A., 49
Windows, story about, 49
Wisdom, 64, 216, 218-20
Work, 28, 221-35

Y

Young, Brigham, 61, 141, 183